Stephen Thraves

*Illustrated by Terry Oakes*

HODDER AND STOUGHTON
LONDON SYDNEY AUCKLAND

British Library Cataloguing in Publication Data

A catalogue record for this book is
available from the British Library

ISBN 0 340 56599 3

Text copyright © Stephen Thraves 1992
Illustrations copyright © Terry Oakes 1992

First published 1992

All rights reserved. No part of this publication may be reproduced or
transmitted in any form or by any means, electronically or mechanically,
including photocpying, recording, or any information storage and
retrieval system, without either prior permission in writing from the
publisher or a licence permitting restricted copying. In the United
Kingdom such licences are issued by the Copyright Licensing Agency,
90 Tottenham Court Road, London W1P 9HE.

The rights of Stephen Thraves to be identified as the author of the text
of this work and of Terry Oakes to be identified as the illustrator of this
work have been asserted by them in accordance with the Copyright,
Designs and Patents Act 1988.

Published by Hodder and Stoughton Children's Books,
a division of Hodder and Stoughton Ltd,
Mill Road, Dunton Green, Sevenoaks, Kent TN13 2YA

Photoset by Rowland Phototypesetting Ltd,
Bury St Edmunds, Suffolk

Printed and bound in Great Britain by
BPCC Hazells Ltd
Member of BPCC Ltd

**W**elcome, fearless one! You have entered the shadowy mythical world of BATTLE QUEST. It is a world of magic and hideous monsters, of treasure and deadly conflict. It is a world where only the most strong, skilful and daring survive. All others perish, forgotten, in its gloom.

Are YOU strong, skilful and daring enough? You will assume the body, mind and courage of a barbarian hero but the dangers that await you will test even your famed abilities to the full. You will have to fight monster warriors of incredible strength; outwit wizards and goblins of exceptional cunning. Tests, traps and deceits lie at every turn. The decisions you make will be gambling with your very life!

Everything you need for your perilous quest is contained within the special wallet. There is one rotating counter to record your increasing or diminishing strength, and another to record how many treasures you have found. There are also various *spell, special powers* and *equipment* cards that are waiting to be picked up at various points in the adventure, and two coloured dice for when battles have to be fought.

Unless you are very lucky, it is unlikely that you will succeed on your very first adventure. You will find that the more times you play, the more skilful you become in making the right decisions and taking the right risks. Your skill-level is represented by the number of treasures you record on the treasure counter and you should aim to keep improving this score until you reach the maximum of *8 treasures*. Only then are you worthy of your great fame!

# BACKGROUND

'So YOU are the famed barbarian warrior!' an old man says, greeting you with a wrinkled, frail hand. He peers at you with his one open eye, but that too seems to be nearly blind. It is dull and crusted. 'They say that your strength has no equal, that your heart knows no fear. Well, we shall see, we shall see. I am Sageor, the lord of this realm.'

Although you have only just arrived on his shore after many weary days at sea, the old man will not allow you so much as a minute's rest. Stumbling and panting, he immediately leads you up the rocky cliff path that climbs above the small stone harbour. 'I wonder,' he says, cackling wheezily into the wind, 'whether it was just the irresistible lure of the challenge that made you answer my plea, or was it rather the prospect of all those treasures? Answer not. It matters neither way to me. As long as I have my revenge!'

At last the old man stops, having led you to the very highest part of the cliffs, right to the sheer edge. He steadies himself against the lashing wind before pointing a gnarled finger out to sea. 'Can you see it?' he demands in emotional croaking voice. 'As far as the eye will travel out to the west. My poor eyes can't see it any more but I can still hear it. I can hear the groans from deep within its evil caverns.'

You peer into the stormy horizon as the old man manically claps his hands to his ears. With you, it's the reverse: you can't hear anything from that direction but you can just about *see* something there. It's the black, jagged silhouette of a sheer-sided island.

'Yes,' your companion says, revealing a yellow-toothed grin as he senses your slight recoil, 'a sight quite terrifying, isn't it? The Island of Fury! The kingdom belonging to Cragcliff, the most merciless ruler that ever was. He uses the island merely for his cruel pleasure, filling its deadly caverns with priceless treasures to lure my young warriors to their doom. I have lost all four of my sons in those caves of his!'

'Not one returned?' you ask with dismay.

'No, not one.' He breaks into a scream, shaking his fist at the

elements. "Tis true my youngest came back but not as he left. His mind has been crazed by what he encountered there, his eyes petrified. From that day since he has never spoken a word. You won't receive any prior assistance there!'

'At least his life wasn't lost,' you remark, trying to console him. 'At least he didn't fail.'

'Of course he failed!' the old man screams again, his long white hair wild in the wind. 'He came back not just empty-headed but empty-handed as well. Not one treasure did he bring back. Oh, it's not for the wealth in itself I say this. But that's how Cragcliff mocks me, don't you see? My sons and warriors either end up dead or completely prizeless. The only way I can wreak revenge is to take those prizes from him – as many as possible!'

So you are now much wiser about why the old man summoned you from all these hundreds of miles away; what precisely he wants from you. He wants you not only to *survive* the terrifying island, but also to *humiliate* the evil Cragcliff by relieving his demon kingdom of as much treasure as you can. It's a double quest.

'Well, will you do it?' the old man asks, a shade calmer now. 'Will you take up the challenge? Your reward is to keep all the treasure you find. Mine is simply to know that my sons haven't died unavenged. Mine is to know that when I next stand atop these cliffs, it will be my laughter that mocks across the waves!'

***Will you agree to venture on this awesome quest? If you do, turn the page . . .***

# QUEST INSTRUCTIONS

## Your strength

1. Before starting your quest at paragraph 1 overleaf, it is necessary to record your starting *strength* on your STRENGTH COUNTER. Your starting strength is six, so turn the counter until **6** shows through the window. Every time you are weakened in some way during the adventure, you must change this number to the next one down. When you reach **0** you are dead and must immediately stop your quest. If you wish to make another attempt at it, you must start the game all over again.

2. There are three ways you can be weakened during the quest. First, as a result of foolishness on your part (drinking a poisonous potion, for example); second, because of strenuous activity; or third, because you have been wounded in battle.

## Fighting battles

3. A battle is fought by simultaneous throwing of the two special dice. The blue dice is YOU, the barbarian hero, armed with *sword* and *shield*. The red dice represents your various monster adversaries: the 'fanged head' representing the *monster* and the scimitar representing its *weapon* or – if it doesn't carry a weapon – its slashing claw or tail.

4. You keep simultaneously throwing the two dice until either you or your monster adversary inflicts a wound. For a wound to be inflicted, one dice must show a weapon uppermost while the other must show the opponent unprotected. Thus, if the blue dice shows the sword and the red dice the monster's head, then *you* have wounded the *monster*. But if the blue dice shows the barbarian and the red dice the scimitar then the *monster* has wounded *you*.

5. Any other combination of the dice (see table overleaf) means that a wound hasn't been inflicted on either side and so you must continue throwing the dice until one has.

6. When a *monster* is wounded, make a mental note of this and then resume the dice-throwing. This is because a monster will always

# QUEST INSTRUCTIONS

fight to the death and you only slay it completely if you are able to inflict a certain number of wounds. That number will vary with each monster and part of the skill of the game is to try to find the monsters that are the least resilient. (So don't be too eager to fight each monster you encounter. You don't have to challenge *every* monster to succeed at the game and others, possibly weaker ones, will often be encountered very soon afterwards.)

7. If *you* are wounded at any point during the battle, however, you must always prudently take flight at once. Thus, you immediately stop the dice-throwing.

### Magic spells, Special powers, Equipment

8. Because the world of BATTLE QUEST is a magical as well as violent one, there are various magic spells and special powers to be gained during your adventures. There are also useful items of equipment to be found. These accessories vary from adventure to adventure but the ones accompanying this particular BATTLE QUEST adventure are: a TRANCE SPELL, INFRA-RED POWER, a PASSWORD SCROLL, and the BOOK OF WISDOM. Possession of these cards will greatly improve the chances of succeeding in your quest and you should therefore make every effort to locate them during the adventure. But until you do locate them, you must keep these four cards face down and out of play.

### Treasure counter

9. The object of the quest is not only to come out of it alive but also to collect as much treasure as possible. You record all treasure collected on the TREASURE COUNTER. Set this at **0** to start with and then try and attain as high a score as possible during the quest. The more times you attempt the quest, the better your score should be. When you have obtained the maximum score of eight treasures, then you have indeed completely mastered the CAVES OF FURY!

# Dice Table

**RED   BLUE**

*Monster* momentarily exposed and you wound it with your *sword*

*Monster's weapon* wounds *you*

*Weapons* clash (i.e. no advantage to either side)

*Monster* strikes but you defend against this with your *shield*

*Monster* momentarily exposed but only your *shield* is to the fore so you're unable to take advantage

Both *monster* and *you* are momentarily exposed but neither side able to take advantage

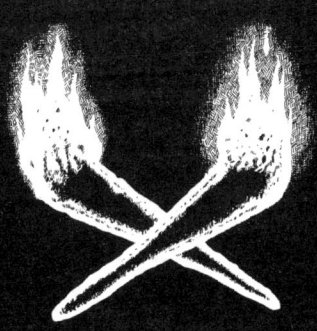

# You are now ready to start. I wish you every luck in your quest and dearly hope that the gods are on your side . . .

# 1

Sageor's wizened silhouette on the cliff-tops becomes smaller and smaller as you row away from his shore. But still he stands there, seeming to watch your gradual progress towards the Island of Fury. Of course, you know that that can't be – his sight reached not so much as a metre in front of him, probably far less than that. You now turn your head the other way and look over your shoulder, trying to make out your destination through the lashing rain. You can just see the island's outline rising sheer and jagged through the swirling dark grey. The storm completely envelopes it for a moment but then the island materialises again, a little clearer this time. Can you now hear those monstrous echoes yourself, you wonder – or is it just the wind ricocheting across the sea? The next plunge of your oars into those violent waves is not before you've had a reassuring glance down at your feet, where lies your trusty broadsword. You row harder and harder, partly because you must if the little rowing-boat is not going to be capsized and partly because the strenuous activity helps detract from your apprehensions. The island is now less than a mile away and you're beginning to make out a trio of chasms close together at the foot of the sheer cliffs. These must be the various entrances to Cragcliff's cavernous kingdom and you consider which one you should steer towards.

> If you prefer left chasm       **go to 209**
> If you prefer right chasm      **go to 335**
> If you prefer central chasm    **go to 84**

## 2

The caves had felt quite chilly until now but, as you follow this branch to the right, the tunnel grows rapidly warmer. It soon feels as if you're walking through a desert, the heat penetrating the soles of your leather boots and making your breathing faster and faster. The perspiration drips from your brow. You wonder at the cause of this sudden change of temperature, but then molten lava, red and glowing, starts to seep up through the cracks and faults in the rocky floor. You break into a run, darting from side to side as the lava collects into tiny streams about your feet. Your whole body is now glistening, your skin wet from the stifling heat and intense exertion, and you start to stumble as your muscles become more and more exhausted.

***Deduct 1 from your STRENGTH RATING. Go next to 238.***

## 3

The whole cave shudders as the brute falls to its knees and then keels over. Its grotesque protruding eyes roll about their sockets and then dart upwards under the warty eyelids. These eyelids flicker a couple of times and then are still. You immediately seize the brute's sword from the ground and smash the blade against a rock to break off the hilt. When you have placed this solid gold handle in your haversack, you make your exit from the cage, squeezing through the stalactites again.

***Add 1 to the score on your TREASURE COUNTER. Now hurry well away from this region by going to 324.***

## 4

Like a dissolving mist, the nebulous apparition slowly disappears, allowing you entry on to the bridge. You quickly cross the stone structure and soon reach the other side where the stepping-stones start again. When you stop and glance back over your shoulder, however, you find that the bridge has mysteriously vanished. It seems to have melted into the swirling green mists, as did its hooded guardian. ***Go to 49.***

## 5

'Cragcliff is the most loathed enemy of us urchins,' the creature rants and screams. 'He hunts us down as feed for his monsters. Ten urchins a day it needs to satisfy just one of them. We were once a thriving breed, dwelling in every single crevice of this island, but Cragcliff's food-hunters have reduced our numbers to less than a couple of thousand.' The incensed creature is about to raise his hand to summon his noxious bats again but you quickly show him the crest in the centre of your shield. ***Go to 254.***

## 6

The brutish voice suddenly roars with cruel laughter. 'We gave you a chance but you still get the password wrong!' it mocks. 'You're no Master Torturer, dog. You can dangle there until you rot!' And it seems that rot you will for you now hear your captors leave the dungeon. The only sounds are the weaker and weaker moans from your fellow prisoner and the occasional creaking of the chain above you. An hour passes – at least it seems a whole hour – then two, and your arms feel as if they are about to tear from their sockets. The strain on them is appalling. Your head starts to sag on to your shoulder, you murmur for water. Your racked body can't take much more.

***Deduct 1 from your STRENGTH RATING. Go next to 146.***

## 7

'Ah, there you are, Tronk, my stupid manservant!' the voice exclaims. 'Caught by the rock-fall were you? Come into my cave of medicines and I'll give you something to restore your strength.' Against the dim light, you can now make out the outline of a small, stooping body behind the voice, apparently clad in the robes of a wizard. But if you can see *him*, he most certainly cannot see *you*. As you take a step forwards, you can see that his eyelids are permanently shut – he's even more blind than Sageor. You decide to take advantage of his mistake and approach the small cave he is beckoning you towards. But the blind old wizard suddenly seems to become suspicious and demands that you give him the correct password from four options he offers you.

*If you have picked up the PASSWORD SCROLL on your adventure, use it here to find out the correct password for the medicine cave. If you don't have the SCROLL, you'll have to guess the correct password.*

| If you think it's GARLON | **go to 241** |
| If you think it's TAGEL | **go to 310** |
| If you think it's KRAVIX | **go to 88** |
| If you think it's RUTHLOR | **go to 46** |

## 8
### THIS CREATURE
### IS SLAIN BY

### WOUNDS

*Wage combat by simultaneously throwing the two dice. If you slay the creature, go to 177. If the creature inflicts a wound on you first, deduct 1 from your STRENGTH RATING and then flee well away from this region by hurrying to 54.*

## 9

You feel your way into the tunnel on the right, wondering when the route will again be illuminated by torchlight. But this must all be part of Cragcliff's campaign of terror because the darkness leads on and on. You round one pitch-black corner after another but still there's no flickering light in front of you. Not even the dimmest glow. *Go to 318.*

## 10

Glancing round, you see an unpleasant-faced goblin standing there, his close-set features scowling at you. 'If you step on that next stone, you will drown!' he calls out frantically. 'Every tenth stone is a trap. Make sure you leap straight over it to the eleventh.' Knowing how malevolent goblins can be, however, you wonder whether he's trying to trick you and it's actually the eleventh stone that's the trap. Maybe he wants to be sure you land on it with as much force as possible.

*If you have been taught the TRANCE SPELL during your adventure, you may cast it here to hypnotise the goblin into telling you whether or not he is speaking the truth about the tenth stepping-stone. To do this, place the TRANCE SPELL card exactly over the goblin's 'mind square' below. If you haven't been taught the TRANCE SPELL, you'll have to hope for the best in deciding what to do.*

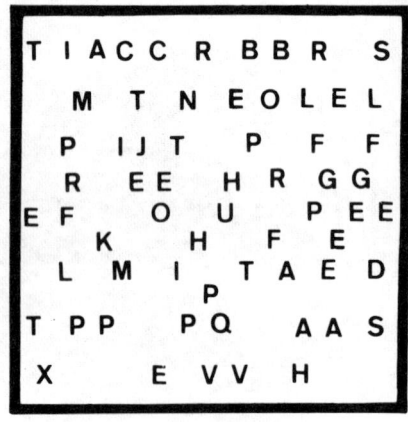

| If you decide to heed goblin's warning | **go to 128** |
|---|---|
| If you decide to ignore it | **go to 320** |

## 11

Your reflection disappears in the ripples caused when you toss the pebble into the pool. You watch the tiny white stone drift and glint to the bottom, waiting for it to have some effect. But you feel no stronger than you were before and so you angrily pick up the other pebble, intending to toss that into the water as well. It's then that your reflection suddenly reappears. 'You were told that you are allowed only one attempt,' it warns, just as you're about to drop the pebble. 'If you toss that one in as well, then you will be weakened even further. So put the pebble back and continue on your way. As long as you don't meet with much more bad luck on your adventure, you may still have just enough strength to complete it.' *Go to 157.*

## 12

The reptile spits saliva furiously in your direction from each of its three mouths as the dwarf orders it back into the tunnel. After another crack of the whip, it is replaced by a second saliva-drooling beast but at least this one only has one head. Hyena-like but much larger, it prowls into the arena with a blood-curdling cackle. It's not

only a vicious-looking beast but also a cunning one. The creature seems to be plotting its tactics already, its yellow slanted eyes narrowing at the sight of you. It swerves deftly to left and right, practising its attacks.

| | |
|---|---|
| If you wish to fight creature | **go to 187** |
| If you wish to avoid it | **go to 263** |

## 13

'Well done!' the hags respond in unison, revealing black teeth as they smile at you. 'You have chosen correctly. For settling our dispute, you must have some of our brew. It will greatly increase your strength.' Although the concoction looks most unappetising, your hunger is intense and so you gratefully accept the ladle they offer you. It's only when you've nearly finished its contents that you suddenly realise that they had continued to stir the cauldron *together*. Didn't they agree that if your guess was right only one of them would stir from now on? So does this mean that it wasn't right after all? That the *other* hag was younger? Unfortunately, it does, because far from feeling a surge of strength in your body you begin to feel a sudden weakening.

***Deduct 1 from your STRENGTH RATING. Go next to 101.***

### 14

As you pass to the left side of the tomb, you keep a suspicious eye on the cast-iron effigy. Is the mummified inhabitant as extinct as the hushed atmosphere suggests or does it still come to life occasionally? Will the tomb's lid suddenly be thrown open and a bandaged hand lash out? But you're now safely past the plinth – and it's not much longer before you are safely out of the strange pyramid altogether. You breathe a grateful sigh of relief, sure that your passage through there was a lot less eventful than it could have been. ***Go to 157.***

### 15

Still very dazed, stars before your eyes, you anxiously grope your way out of the Chief Sorcerer's cave. You stumble and slide down to the bottom of the large cavern again, fearing that at any moment the next monster will appear before you. You practice wielding your sword but you seem to have lost all control over it, flapping the weapon uselessly at the air. You are just about to sink to your knees in desperation when an invisible hand slips into yours. *Go to 163.*

## 16
## THIS CREATURE
## IS SLAIN BY

## WOUNDS

*Wage combat by simultaneously throwing the two dice. If you slay the creature, go to 333. If the creature inflicts a wound on you first, deduct 1 from your STRENGTH RATING and then flee well away from this region by hurrying to 109.*

## 17
As the creature hits the ground it suddenly turns to stone again and shatters into a thousand pieces. You look round at these, searching desperately for the emerald. You spot it at last, glinting, some distance apart from the bulk of the rubble. There's still a piece of the stone sword round it but you chip it away with another fragment of stone. You then carefully put the emerald into your haversack.

*Add 1 to the score on your TREASURE COUNTER. Now hurry well away from this region by going to 109.*

## 18
You peer into the cave to see how deep it is but it's pitch black inside. Unable to tell what traps might lie in there, you decide it would be prudent to continue past it. But you're just about to start moving again when a delicious smell reaches your nostrils. It's the smell of roasting meat – possibly wild boar. You haven't eaten for

many hours and your hunger tempts you closer to the dark opening. Dare you enter that blackness or is the delicious waft just an illusory one to lure you to a horrible death?

*If you have acquired INFRA-RED POWER during your adventure, you may employ it here to find out whether the cave is safe or not. Place the INFRA-RED POWER CARD exactly over the 'cave entrance' below. If you haven't acquired INFRA-RED POWER, you'll have to hope for the best in making your decision.*

If you wish to enter cave    **go to 216**
If you wish to ignore it     **go to 138**

### 19

You've crawled only a short distance through the shaft on the left when you feel something trail across your back. It's just a dangling tendril so you ignore it. But then the tendril suddenly starts to wrap itself around you. Kicking out, you easily crawl free of it but then another coils round you – and another. They're everywhere now, grabbing at your wrists, ankles and neck. You start to crawl for all you are worth, badly grazing your elbows and knees, in a desperate attempt to escape them. But the tendrils seem to become more and more, thicker and thicker. At last you reach the end of the shaft –

arriving at the main tunnel again, where you were before. But it's with all the breath squeezed out of you and in a state of total exhaustion.

***Deduct 1 from your STRENGTH RATING. Go next to 330.***

## 20

Now on the far side of the chasm, you are about to continue your journey when you notice a gigantic nest on a rocky ledge below you. There's an egg inside – but no ordinary egg. It appears to be of solid gold. Sure that you can reach it, you carefully lie down at the very edge of the chasm and stretch out your hand. Your fingers are just about to wrap round it when a monstrous bird flies up from the

depths. It is quite hideous, with a featherless skull for a head and huge blood-dripping claws. You realise that if the egg is to be yours, you will have to take this creature on.

| | |
|---|---|
| If you wish to fight the creature | **go to 161** |
| If you wish to avoid it | **go to 87** |

## 21

The violent water tosses you to this side and that, several times nearly dragging you under, but your strong arms continue steering against its awesome power. Finally, though, your arms tire and the struggle becomes an impossible one. Just as you're resigning yourself to your fate, however, the whirlpool starts to subside. Before very long the water has completely disappeared and you find yourself lying on the rocky floor of the chasm. You were lucky . . . but all that exertion has taken a considerable toll on your strength.

***Deduct 1 from your STRENGTH RATING. Go next to 194.***

## 22

'So you chose correctly!' the strange little man shouts to you across the bridge. 'But how do I know that it wasn't just a lucky guess? I have one more test for you just to make sure. In the middle of the bridge you will see that there are three small wooden chests. Walk right up to them.' You do as he instructs, seeing that all the box-lids are beautifully carved with an intricate design of vines and birds. 'You must open one of these,' the mason continues. 'If you open either of the two wrong ones, your strength will be greatly reduced.'

***If you have picked up the BOOK OF WISDOM during your adventure, you may consult it here to find out which is the correct chest to open. If you haven't, you'll have to hope for the best in making your decision.***

| | |
|---|---|
| If you choose left chest | **go to 305** |
| If you choose centre chest | **go to 332** |
| If you choose right chest | **go to 104** |

## 23

In the pit you find a series of hand and foot holds to help you climb down to the bottom. It's not as far down as you were expecting; only three or four metres. Your shield is lying right in front of you and, just to make absolutely sure it *is* your shield, you knock it against the icy wall of the pit. The metal rings reassuringly! ***Go to 74.***

## 24

'What are you doing, fools?' you shout at your unseen tormentors. 'I am the new Master Torturer come to these dungeons. Release me immediately!' Your ploy seems to have some effect because you can sense a slight confusion in front of you. 'If you are who you say you are,' a brutish voice asks uncertainly, 'then what is the password for these dungeons?'

*If you have picked up the PASSWORD SCROLL in your adventure, use it here to find out the correct password for the torture dungeons. If you don't have the SCROLL, you'll have to guess the password.*

| If you think it's QUADEN | **go to 6** |
| If you think it's NURLAT | **go to 175** |
| If you think it's SILLAR | **go to 269** |
| If you think it's PHENDON | **go to 317** |

## 25

You haven't followed the right branch of the tunnel very far when you think you hear sniffing echoing from some distance behind you. But then it disappears and you put it out of your mind. A few minutes later, though, you hear the sound again. It's much clearer this time and you realise that the sniffing is coming from a pack of bloodhounds. They seem to be closing in on you at every step and you anxiously wonder whether you will be able to outrun them. *Go to 229.*

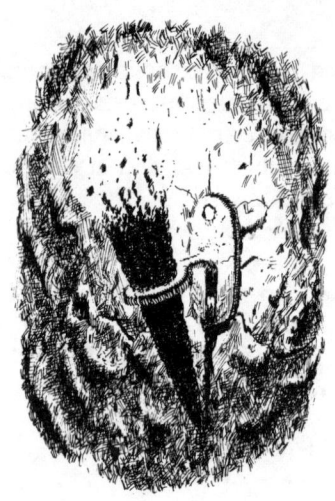

## 26

You put the dwarf's arena further and further behind as another dimly lit tunnel snakes away in front of you. But it's not long before the echoes tell you that a second large cavern is just ahead. There's a steady red glow from this cavern that becomes stronger and stronger as you approach. Soon you are standing at the entrance to the cavern – although there are in fact three entrances, all arched and of equal size. The rock between the arches has been exquisitely chiselled, decorated with birds and lifelike nymphs, and there's an ornate inscription above the middle arch. It reads: *You stand before the hall of mysteries. Enter with respect. Enter with wisdom too. Two of these three arches hide evil. Only one will cause you no harm. Choose wisely.*

**If you have picked up the BOOK OF WISDOM in your adventure, you may consult it here to find out which of the three entrances is the harmless one. If you haven't, you'll have to hope for the best in making your decision.**

| | |
|---|---|
| If you choose left arch | **go to 132** |
| If you choose centre arch | **go to 179** |
| If you choose right arch | **go to 290** |

## 27

The moment you have uttered the password the misty face wafts to one side and then disintegrates. You assume from this that your password must have been correct and you step into the ice cavern. Suddenly, however, there's an ominous rumbling sound from the huge ledges of ice above. Fearing that there's about to be some sort of avalanche, you try and run for cover. But your leather boots slip on the glacial floor of the cavern and you crash to the ground. Seconds later, the ledge of ice crashes to the ground as well, piling on top of you. Do you still have enough strength to claw your way out?

*Deduct 1 from your STRENGTH RATING. Go next to 147.*

## 28
## THIS CREATURE
## IS SLAIN BY

## WOUNDS

*Wage combat by simultaneously throwing the two dice. If you slay the creature, go to 72. If the creature inflicts a wound on you first, deduct 1 from your STRENGTH RATING and then flee well away from this region by hurrying to 136.*

## 29

Passing through the ice door on the left, you hope to feel a sudden surge of strength. But there's nothing. You feel no stronger than you were before. You wonder whether you should re-enter the temple so you can come out by one of the other doors. But you decide against it. Having already experienced their deceptive power, you daren't risk provoking the prophetesses into even greater resentment against you. *Go to 74.*

## 30

As you are walking through the tunnel, you suddenly feel drips falling on your shoulder. Is this the trap you'd been fearing, you wonder anxiously. Are those drips poison? When you feel round above your head, however, you are relieved to discover that there are only icicles up there. The fact that they are dripping is good news; it proves that the caves are gradually getting warmer. But *are* the drips such good news? For you suddenly feel a burning sensation on your shoulder and you start to feel strangely giddy . . .

***Deduct 1 from your STRENGTH RATING. Go next to 325.***

## 31

The creature's death-howl is as terrifying as the way it fought. The whole cavern echoes with the hideous sound as it doubles up on the ground, clasping its last and fatal wound. Finally, though, it is quiet and still – and you now tentatively peer into the tomb from which the creature emerged. You're expecting a thick layer of foul-smelling decay in there but it's empty. Empty that is except for the beautiful gold chalice in one corner.

***Add 1 to the score on your TREASURE COUNTER. Now hurry well away from this region by going to 136.***

## 32
## THIS CREATURE
## IS SLAIN BY

## WOUNDS

*Wage combat by simultaneously throwing the two dice. If you slay the creature, go to 323. If the creature inflicts a wound on you first, deduct 1 from your STRENGTH RATING and then flee well away from this region by rowing to 120.*

### 33
After a brief rest you leave the pair of holes behind you, following the tunnel again. It's not long before it joins with another tunnel emerging from your left and you guess that this is one of those other branches that you could have taken. And it's not much longer after *that* that this wider tunnel comes to a deep chasm. This is crossed by two narrow stone bridges; one to your left and one to your right. You're just wondering which is the safest when a strange little man appears behind you. *Go to 112.*

### 34
'Enter handsome stranger,' says one as her hooded eyes suddenly notice you there. 'You can settle our dispute. We both agree that the

cauldron should be stirred by the one who is the younger. I say it is me, she says it is her. Tell us which one is right and we'll argue no more. Get it wrong and you shall pay.'

*If you have been taught the **TRANCE SPELL** during your adventure, you may cast it here to hypnotise the hags into admitting which one is lying about being the younger. To do this, place the **TRANCE SPELL CARD** exactly over their 'mind square' below. If you haven't been taught the **TRANCE SPELL**, you'll have to hope for the best in making your decision.*

| If you think hag on left is lying | **go to 13** |
| If you think hag on right is lying | **go to 250** |

### 35

Your boat slowly enters the arch on the right, conveying you into a long, straight tunnel. You're hoping at any moment to spot a pin-prick of daylight at the end of this but the darkness remains total. For a long while the only sound is the quiet paddling of your oars but then a strange wailing starts to echo towards you. It becomes more and more high-pitched, louder and louder, very soon deafening you. Desperately, you clasp your hands to your ears to try and block it out. The shrill wail seems to be penetrating right to your very brain. At last it starts to subside but the hideous sound leaves you trembling, feeling strangely weak . . .

*Deduct 1 from your STRENGTH RATING. Go next to 293.*

## 36

Yes, *that's* how . . . for this time you notice a dark pit a few metres to one side of your path. At the bottom there's a manic, yellow-eyed skeleton, brandishing a sword at you. The belligerent creature appears to be trapped down there so you could easily avoid taking up its challenge. But then you notice the large ruby embedded in its

spiked helmet. You also notice a long coil of rope anchored to the edge of the pit. This would enable you to climb down into the pit – and then leave it again if you managed to slay the monster. The rope was obviously left here by Cragcliff as an invitation. Will you take up that invitation, though?

| | |
|---|---|
| If you wish to fight skeleton | **go to 141** |
| If you wish to avoid it | **go to 172** |

## 37

Slowly opening the chest in the middle, you're amazed to discover that it's completely empty. You can't understand it. When you shook the chest you heard something roll round inside. The face in the water starts to laugh at you – and you now realise whose features they are. They belong to that wizard! 'You chose an empty chest,' he explains contemptuously. 'It rattled only because I made it rattle. You shouldn't have tried to cheat!' ***Go to 312.***

## 38

As luck would have it, there are two ropes dangling a short distance ahead of you, about three metres apart. Each leads up to a large hole in the roof of the tunnel. The holes are pitch-black, though, and as you stare upwards, first at one, then the other, you wonder if there might be any danger up there.

***If you have acquired INFRA-RED POWER during your adventure, you may employ it here to see through the darkness of each hole in the roof. To do this, place the INFRA-RED POWER CARD exactly over their 'black openings' below. If you don't have INFRA-RED POWER, you'll have to hope for the best in making your decision.***

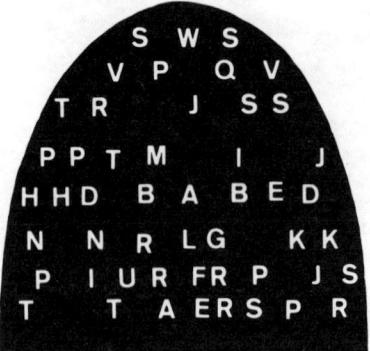
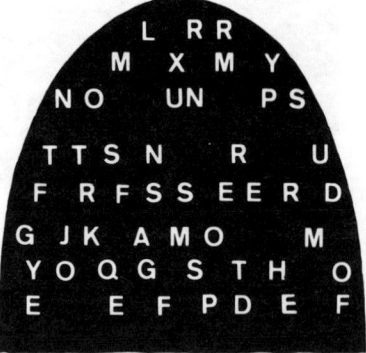

If you choose left roof hole      **go to 316**
If you choose right roof hole      **go to 188**

## 39

At last you can see daylight ahead! At first it's just a small dot but then the whitish grey patch becomes larger and larger. You feel invigorated by the sight, not even daunted by the long sea voyage that is to follow. Suddenly the rock all about you starts to vibrate with a booming voice. It's the voice of Cragcliff himself! 'So you have survived all my traps and terrors,' he laughs monstrously. 'Both your body and mind are intact. But I have one last prize for you – the central diamond from my crown. It's the largest and most precious jewel ever found. For it to be yours, you must fight one more of my creatures. This is your very last challenge.' The renewed laughter that follows, however, makes it quite clear that it will also be the hardest! *Go to 207.*

## 40
### THIS CREATURE
### IS SLAIN BY

### WOUNDS

*Wage combat by simultaneously throwing the two dice. If you slay the creature, go to 3. If the creature inflicts a wound on you first, deduct 1 from your STRENGTH RATING and then flee well away from this region by hurrying to 324.*

## 41

Having made sure your rowing-boat is pulled well up the shore, beyond the level of the tides, you now tentatively approach the huge chasm. It emits a hideous wailing sound, dispelling any lingering doubts that you might have as to whether this is one of the entrances to Cragcliff's kingdom. The whole island seems to shudder with the sound and sea-birds scream their fright in the bleak skies far above. You had already noticed how none of the birds cares to fly too close to this land. Gripping your sword even tighter, pulse racing, you now enter the first shadows of the chasm. Venturing further in, you suddenly hear the sound of water gurgling at your feet. The sea has somehow risen from underground and a foaming whirlpool quickly swells round you, rising higher and higher. It's soon at the level of your thighs and you realise that you had better take action before the water sucks you under. What will you do?

| Try and wade quickly through the whirlpool | **go to 240** |
| Clamber up on to the rocks at the edge | **go to 267** |
| Quickly make your way back | **go to 85** |

### 42

The urchin points to three chests in the corner of his small cave. 'One of those chests contains an antidote to the stench that you have inhaled from my bats,' he says. 'I can't tell you more because I am enchanted by an evil sorcerer. If I disclose which is the right chest, then my bats will turn against me and devour all but my left thumb.' The ceiling of the cave is low, so on hands and knees you crawl over to the chests. You notice that all these lids have been carved with ornate flowers and vines. Which should you open?

*If you have picked up the BOOK OF WISDOM during your adventure, you may consult it here to find out which is the correct chest. If you haven't, you'll have to hope for the best in making your decision.*

| If you choose left chest | **go to 190** |
| If you choose centre chest | **go to 226** |
| If you choose right chest | **go to 257** |

### 43

As you lie back on the beach, you wonder whether you are right to delay entering the chasm. The longer you leave it, the more your courage is likely to falter. On the other hand, you feel quite exhausted after all that strenuous rowing and you want to be sure that you enter the chasm as refreshed as possible. So you compromise by deciding to rest for only ten minutes. It's not an easy rest, though. Every time you shut your eyes and try to clear your mind, you hear yet another screech or howl from that gaping hole behind you. It's almost as if the multitude of monsters in there are aware of your arrival, eagerly and malevolently preparing themselves. ***Go to 122.***

**44**

Little wonder that the goblin was anxious to be off because no sooner have you yelled out Cragcliff's name a second time than a distant part of the swamp erupts. It's as if a giant mouth has sucked at it, lifting the muddy mass up from its very depths. But then you realise that the massive cone of slime isn't the swamp erupting at all, for now it begins to move towards you! The grotesque creature

underneath the muddy coating becomes clearer and clearer at every step as the long tendrils of slime drip away from it. First you can see its hideous bulging eyes, then you can distinguish its scaly body.

And you can also make out the dazzling ruby at the base of its sword, shining like a red fire through all the clinging slime . . .

If you wish to fight creature   **go to 8**
If you wish to avoid it        **go to 215**

## 45

As you continue to follow the torch-lit path, the flickering yellow shadows dancing dimly round one corner after another, you wonder what Cragcliff has next in store for you. You're sure that your encounters so far have only been an introduction to his monstrous kingdom; a relatively tame prelude to the terrors that lie further in. You're sure that this tunnel is eventually going to open up into much larger chambers where your nightmarish adventures will begin for real. For the moment, though, the tunnel continues its narrow course, although it does soon branch three ways. Which branch should you follow?

If you prefer branch on left    **go to 164**
If you prefer branch to right   **go to 2**
If you prefer branch in middle  **go to 249**

## 46

'Ah, so you are *not* so stupid, Tronk!' the funny little creature sniggers. 'You can still remember the password I gave you. Come inside and I will make you up a medicine that will instantly heal the blow to your head.' You do as he asks but when you see all the putrid-looking bottles and jars lining the shelves in his caves, you wonder how reliable a healer he is. Many of the bottles have mould growing inside them and the contents of the jars closely resemble festering animal organs. But if you're going to complete this quest, you need every bit of fortitude you can get and so you decide to trust him. You try not to retch as you watch the wizard make up a cocktail for you – the contents of two of these bottles in a goblet, stirred together with his grimy finger. He tells you to down the fermenting slime in one. As foul as it tastes, you can immediately feel your head clear and some of the power return to your weakened body.

*Add 1 to your STRENGTH RATING. Go next to 145.*

### 47

'Your password is correct, youth,' the wizard tells you after you have said it in a disguised voice, raising the pitch a little. Fortunately, he still doesn't turn round and you decide to continue with the deception to see what you might learn from him. He might teach you something that will be of invaluable assistance in your quest. *Go to 326.*

### 48
### THIS CREATURE
### IS SLAIN BY

⟨2⟩

### WOUNDS

*Wage combat by simultaneously throwing the two dice. If you slay the creature, go to 198. If the creature inflicts a wound on you first, deduct 1 from your STRENGTH RATING and then flee well away from this region by hurrying to 26.*

## 49

After a brief rest, you continue to follow the stepping-stones across the swamp, the swirling mists becoming thicker and thicker. Soon you can see no more than a few metres in front of you and the only sound is the pestilent one of mosquitoes. They whine all about you in the putrid green vapours. As you persevere on your journey, you again wonder how deep the swamp is. The existence of the stepping-stones would suggest it is quite shallow, but you know how false that assumption is likely to be. The stones might have infinite depth and the thought sobers you, making you certain not to lose your balance. The snaking path suddenly provides you with another problem, though – for it branches three ways. Which branch should you take?

| If left branch | **go to 339** |
| If middle branch | **go to 171** |
| If right branch | **go to 134** |

## 50

As you continue your journey through the caves, following yet another shadowy tunnel, the air seems to grow a lot colder. You wish you had brought an animal skin to drape over your shoulders. Wisps of icy vapour start to waft towards you; pale blue streaks mingling with the dark. You eventually reach the source of these frozen breaths of air as the tunnel suddenly opens up into a huge cavern. Icicles hang everywhere, their glistening reflections providing a natural illumination. And the floor of the chamber is not rock, but wastes of sparkling glacier. There seems to be the light of a thousand candles; and yet not one is evident there. ***Go to 139.***

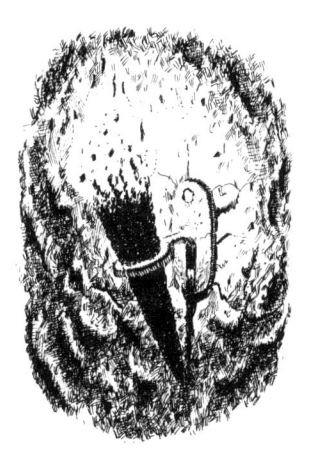

### 51

As you follow the goblin's advice and step off the stones to wade through the swamp, you wonder how wisely you have acted. Even if he isn't the same as that first creature you encountered, what's to say he isn't as wicked? Just because he was telling the truth about his identity it doesn't mean that he was also telling the truth in his advice. Malice is surely in every goblin's nature. But it seems there wasn't any trickery, for the swamp is shallow at this part. And soon you're completely reassured, for behind you the stepping-stones suddenly catch fire, one after the other, their flames leaping high into the air. Had you not left them, your quest would have come to an abrupt end. ***Go to 106.***

### 52

Moving along to the next statue, you read exactly the same inscription there: *Beware! If any part of this statue be touched, the creature will immediately come to life.* Above the inscription a tall monster-warrior stares down at you with manic eyes in a bony head. Its bony claws end in long, sharp nails and the nails on the right claw are wrapped round a huge curved sword. You step a little closer to the stone sword to see if there is a jewel set in that one as well. Disappointed that you can't see one, you're about to move on from

the statue when you peer up at the monster's staring eyes again. The one staring back at you on the right is a large diamond! In wonder you almost touch the statue – but you jump back in time. You should, of course, only touch it if you intend to fight it.

> If you wish to fight creature **go to 16**
> If you wish to avoid it **go to 191**

### 53

Your arms growing weaker and weaker as they flail at the sucking mud, you suddenly hear the goblin's high-pitched voice again above you. He's on a raft, punting across the swamp towards you. You try to grab his punt-pole to haul yourself out but he teasingly keeps yanking it back just out of your reach. 'Oh, no you don't!' his hideous squeal taunts. 'I've come to watch you drown, stranger!' ***Go to 160.***

## 54

The swamp is now mercifully well behind you as you continue your journey into the depths of the island. The rocky walls start to narrow once more, the echo of the drips becoming shorter. It's little more than a wide tunnel you're following, turning sharply to left and right. Suddenly you come to a dead-end, a flank of damp rock right across your path. But then, to your relief, you notice a series of steps roughly cut into the rock. The tunnel merely continues at a higher level. You're just about to climb these steps when you see that there are some more, a few metres to your right. They must lead to another higher branch of the tunnel. Which set of steps should you take?

> If you prefer steps in front    **go to 327**
> If you prefer steps to the right    **go to 201**

## 55

Miraculously, the long drop doesn't kill you. There's a pool of water at the bottom of the chasm, just deep enough to break your fall. You are very badly shaken by your terrifying plunge but at least your quest doesn't come to an abrupt end. Or does it? How are you going to climb out of this deep chasm? The sides are sheer; they would be impossible to climb even if you hadn't been weakened by the fall, let alone now that you have. It's then that you notice two large, pitch-black arches in the rock. ***Go to 217.***

## 56

You quickly drop the book into your haversack, hoping that the cook wasn't sharp enough to notice which you chose. All the time you are gnawing at your hunk of meat you wonder whether your choice was a good one. The bottom book was certainly a very heavy one – and that's just what you would expect the *Book of Wisdom* to be. It was also very old-looking and you would expect the *Book of Wisdom* to be that as well. Its leather-bound covers were crumbling and scarred and its pages seemed frail and yellowing. You daren't make absolutely sure, though, until you have bade the cook farewell and put his cave some distance behind you. When you at last take out the heavy volume and hold its engraved title up to the nearest flickering torch, you're horrified to read: *Methods of Spit-Roasting*. **Go to 93.**

## 57

For a long time it looks as if your search along the narrow stretch of shingle is in vain. But then you notice an old bottle amongst the rocks at the water's edge. It's amazing that the bottle hasn't been smashed to smithereens by the fierce lashing of the waves but it's completely intact. And inside is a roll of parchment. You quickly break the bottle to extract the parchment and discover a series of what appear to be passwords written on it. You wonder if these are passwords to some of Cragcliff's caves. Sure that they must be, you try to memorise as many of them as you can before putting the scroll into your haversack.

***You may pick up the PASSWORD SCROLL. Go next to 122.***

## 58

The cavern that you wander into from the arch is by far the largest you have encountered in this maze of tunnels and caves. No wonder its red glow could be seen from so far away. The glow is made up from the light of thousands of candles that flicker away in here, its hue red because of the strange rock colour. It's the shade of blood. But, despite the candles, the cavern is still a place of many shadows, nooks and crannies honeycombing its steep sides. It's those nooks and crannies – dark, concealing and mysterious – that presumably give this place its name. You decide without further ado to explore this Hall of Mysteries, wondering whether you should take a route to the left, the right or the centre.

| | |
|---|---|
| If you prefer left | **go to 276** |
| If you prefer right | **go to 309** |
| If you prefer centre | **go to 143** |

## 59

Having climbed the few steps up to the bottom row of tombs, you squeeze along to the first cave. The candle flickers as you enter, your shadow for a moment hesitant on the rough cold wall. The large stone tomb lies still and quiet in the cave's centre and you cautiously approach it, wondering what sort of monstrous creation it contains. There is an effigy of the slain warrior on top of the tomb. As you touch this stone warrior, however, it miraculously starts to change. The serene and noble head transforms into a grotesque, horned skull. The small horns seem to sprout everywhere; from the

brow, the cheeks, the jaws. The warrior's weapon also starts to change; the broadsword lying at his side turning into a vicious scimitar. You now know the demon you will encounter if you open this tomb. But you keep thinking about the treasure that you have been told lies inside . . .

>    If you wish to fight creature    **go to 251**
>    If you wish to avoid it    **go to 129**

### 60

You tread with great care as you enter the arch on the right. You know that deadly asps and cobras often lurk in pyramids. But it's not your legs that you suddenly find entangled – it's your head. And the trap comes not in the form of a writhing snake but a huge spider's web. You desperately try to free yourself from this clinging web but it has a thread of pliable steel, thick and strong. Your sword is quite useless against it. You've now fallen to the floor in your frantic efforts to claw it off and you're convinced that the enveloping mesh is about to finish you. It starts to tighten round your neck. But then, suddenly, it begins to unwrap itself again, falling away in limp shreds. Half-throttled, you're left gasping desperately for air.

*Deduct 1 from your STRENGTH RATING. Go next to 256.*

### 61
As you utter your chosen password, so does your reflection. It then starts to speak independently of you again. 'You have chosen correctly,' it says without expression, without showing the relief that you are sure *you* must be showing. 'You may now walk away from this pool and continue on your adventure.' *Go to 157.*

### 62
You tread with great caution as you make your way through the exit. The pitcher might be on the floor of the arch and you don't want to kick it over in case it's fragile or unsealed. But, as it turns out, the pitcher seems to be neither on the floor nor anywhere else in the arch, for you reach the outside of the pyramid without finding it. *Go to 157.*

## 63
## THIS CREATURE
## IS SLAIN BY

<9>

### WOUNDS

*Wage combat by simultaneously throwing the two dice. If you slay the creature, go to 234. If the creature inflicts a wound on you first, deduct 1 from your STRENGTH RATING and then flee well away from this region by hurrying to 136.*

### 64

You scramble up into the hole and haul in the rope just in time. A moment or two later the bloodhounds are passing directly beneath you. There's at least a dozen of them and they are monstrous, the size of deer. You anxiously hold your breath as the hounds hesitate, having suddenly lost your scent trail. At one point one looks up at your refuge with rabid, yellow eyes but then, to your relief, it looks away again, bewildered. You hear their handler shout at them. 'Dumb beasts!' he snarls bad-temperedly, yanking their leads to turn them round. 'I told you there was no one down this tunnel. As punishment, there'll be no scraps when you get back!' ***Go to 33.***

## 65

Admiring these carvings, the delicate flowers and nymphs, you decide to open one of the chests. But then an ill-defined face appears where your left oar drips into the water. It starts to speak, rippling slightly. 'Consider a while before you investigate any of the chests,' it warns. 'One of them contains a magic potion that will restore some of your strength. But you must open this chest *first*.'

***If you have picked up the BOOK OF WISDOM during your adventure, you may consult it here to find out which is the right chest to open. If not, you'll have to hope for the best in making your decision.***

| | |
|---|---|
| If you choose chest on left | **go to 115** |
| If you choose chest in centre | **go to 37** |
| If you choose chest on right | **go to 282** |

## 66

Fortunately, there do not appear to be any more portcullises to hinder your journey down this tunnel. That one sturdy gate at the beginning must have been considered enough. But although the long, twisting passageway doesn't present any further impediments, it soon presents you with a difficult decision, for it suddenly branches into three. You hope there might be a chiselled inscription somewhere in the rock to advise you which branch to take. But there's nothing – not even a chalked arrow. So you'll just have to take a chance on which is the best route to follow.

| | |
|---|---|
| If you choose left branch | **go to 274** |
| If you choose middle branch | **go to 142** |
| If you choose right branch | **go to 25** |

## 67

Deciding to avoid the mercenary, you steer the boat away from the right bank, taking a course nearer to the left one. But then a creature suddenly appears on this side of the river too. It emerges from a shadowy cave, a gigantic mace in its right hand. It swings the heavy club in huge, terrifying arcs above its ape-like head. This creature looks as if it will be a very formidable opponent; one almost impossible to beat. But dare you let pass another chance to win Cragcliff's diamond?

| | |
|---|---|
| If you wish to fight creature | **go to 169** |
| If you wish to avoid it | **go to 120** |

## 68

This stairway through the rock is the strangest you've ever encountered. You have climbed only about a dozen steps when you emerge at the top of the chasm again, which works out at a height of only three or four metres. But surely you had fallen at least ten times that distance! *Go to 20.*

**69**

You notice that the tunnel has mysteriously become dry once more. You are just about to leave the urchin's cave when he suddenly turns nasty again. 'How do I know that you haven't tricked me?' he demands suspiciously. 'Cragcliff's food hunters could have changed the crest on their shields just to root out us remaining urchins? To prove you are who you say you are you must pass a test.' *Go to 174.*

**70**

But your relief is short lived. For, though little do you realise it, standing in the shadows behind you is a goblin. He's furious that you have climbed up into his home. As you crouch over the hole to make sure the hounds have completely disappeared below, he pushes you hard in the back. You fall helplessly through the air, landing head first in the tunnel.

*Deduct 1 from your STRENGTH RATING. Go next to 33.*

**71**
**THIS CREATURE**
**IS SLAIN BY**

◇ 8 ◇

**WOUNDS**

*Wage combat by simultaneously throwing the two dice. If you slay the creature, go to 253. If the creature inflicts a wound on you first, deduct 1 from your STRENGTH RATING and then flee well away from the region by hurrying to 45.*

**72**

The creature staggers back from the final thrust of your sword, baring its fangs as it howls in agony. In one last desperate attempt, it raises its fiery sword high above its head, intending to hurl it at you. But the sword drops limply behind its back, and is extinguished as it hits the ground. You now lift the lid of the tomb right off and reach inside for that leather pouch. Will it contain gold coins or jewels? It's the latter; at least thirty perfect diamonds!

*Add 1 to the score on your TREASURE COUNTER. Now hurry well away from this region by going to 136.*

### 73
### THIS CREATURE IS SLAIN BY

### ⟨9⟩

### WOUNDS

*Wage combat by simultaneously throwing the two dice. If you slay the creature, go to 328. If the creature inflicts a wound on you first, deduct 1 from your STRENGTH RATING and then flee well away from this region by hurrying to 136.*

### 74

It's not much longer before you have made your way to the far side of the ice cavern. Here you find a narrow tunnel. As you follow this, you are relieved to discover that the air is gradually becoming warmer again. You now wonder what else Cragcliff has in store for you. Is it another hostile environment – perhaps extreme heat this time – or are there to be more of his monstrous creatures? It's little wonder that no one has ever survived his caves. *Go to 325.*

## 75

Deciding to ignore this second creature as well, you now cautiously move towards the cage on the left to investigate *its* treasure and monstrous guard. Your eyes can't help but fix on the monster first. It's a minotaur, a creature which has the head of a bull and the body of a tall man. The shoulders are wide and muscular and it is these

which seem to prevent the beast from slipping between the stalactite pillars as it thrusts its head towards you, its hands grasping for you. Your eyes start to search the cage for the treasure the minotaur protects. It takes a while for you to realise that you had been staring at it all the time! Through the creature's frenziedly-snorting nose is a ring of solid gold.

| | |
|---|---|
| If you wish to fight creature | **go to 107** |
| If you wish to ignore it | **go to 324** |

## 76

'Your password is correct,' the wizard says, unmooring the boat for you. 'It will not be much longer now before you reach the outside.

You will find yourself on the opposite side of the island to the cove you landed at but this craft is much stronger than your own and so there will be no loss. Forget your own boat and use this one to return to the land you came from. I wish you luck on the remainder of your journey.' *Go to 189.*

### 77

Your apprehensions are justified because, when you come right up to the bridge, the mists strangely start to gather in front of you, forming into a vague hooded figure. 'To cross this bridge requires the correct password,' the misty apparition murmurs at you from under its deep hood. 'It is one of three: *Nurlat, Quaden* or *Sillar*. Choose now or turn back whence you came.'

*If you have picked up the PASSWORD SCROLL on your adventure, use it here to find out the correct password to cross the bridge. If you don't have the SCROLL, you'll have to make a guess at it.*

| | |
|---|---|
| If you think it's NURLAT | **go to 212** |
| If you think it's QUADEN | **go to 4** |
| If you think it's SILLAR | **go to 170** |

### 78
**THIS CREATURE
IS SLAIN BY**

⟨**3**⟩

**WOUNDS**

*Wage combat by simultaneously throwing the two dice. If you slay the creature, go to 323. If the creature inflicts a wound on you first, deduct 1 from your STRENGTH RATING and then flee well away from this region by hurrying to 120.*

## 79
## THIS CREATURE IS SLAIN BY

◇9◇

## WOUNDS

*Wage combat by simultaneously throwing the two dice. If you slay the creature, go to 336. If the creature inflicts a wound on you first, deduct 1 from your STRENGTH RATING and then flee well away from this region by hurrying to 54.*

## 80
Following the mermaid's instruction, you keep as far to the right side of the river as you can. Although the current is still very strong here, it's not violent enough to turn your boat over. Indeed, you're almost grateful for it because it conveys your boat much more quickly than your oars could have done. After some quarter of a mile of this rough water, the river suddenly grows calmer again. There surely can't be much further to go now. ***Go to 39.***

## 81
'Stop!' the goblin screams at you as you raise your sword at him, determined to put an end to his malicious pleasures once and for all. 'I have done you no harm. I can see from the anger on your face that

you have encountered my wicked twin, have you not? But I am not like him. I have merely come to advise you to step off the stones and wade the rest of the way through the swamp.' You scrutinise the goblin as you consider this advice. He looks absolutely identical to the other, with the same pinched, evil-looking features. *Is* he the good twin? Or are they one and the same?

*If you have been taught the TRANCE SPELL during your adventure, you may cast it here to hypnotise the goblin into telling you whether he is speaking the truth or not about being the other's twin. To do this, place the TRANCE SPELL CARD exactly over the goblin's 'mind square' below. If you haven't been taught the TRANCE SPELL you'll have to hope for the best in deciding whether to accept his advice or not.*

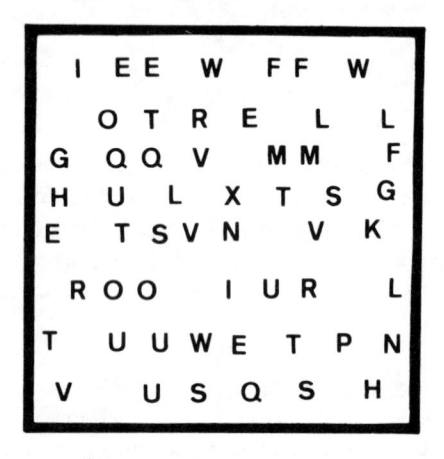

```
  I   E E   W   F F   W

      O T R   E     L     L
  G   Q Q V     M M       F
  H   U L X   T   S       G
  E   T S V N     V       K

      R O O   I U R       L

  T   U U W E   T   P     N
  V     U S Q   S         H
```

If you decide to follow his advice       **go to 51**
If you decide to ignore it                **go to 159**


### 82
The table is also thrown into darkness by the fire and you're able to sit there, confident that the cook still can't see you. 'How is everything at Cragcliff's court?' the cook chats amiably as he brings the delicious-smelling joint to your table. 'One hears very little

being so far removed from it. Oh, that reminds me. Cragcliff's chief wizard left his *Book of Wisdom* last time he came this way. It's on that shelf there. Perhaps you could return it to him for me?' Of course, you would be delighted to take away the *Book of Wisdom* . . . but which of the large books on the shelf is it? There are three lying there. The cook seems to expect you to know what the *Book of Wisdom* looks like and so you daren't flick through each of them in case it alerts his suspicion. You'll just have to guess the correct book to pick up. Which will you choose?

| If the top book on the pile | **go to 337** |
| If the middle book | **go to 130** |
| If the bottom book | **go to 56** |

### 83
## THIS CREATURE IS SLAIN BY

◇ 9 ◇

## WOUNDS

*Wage combat by simultaneously throwing the two dice. If you slay the creature, go to 308. If the creature inflicts a wound on you first, deduct 1 from your STRENGTH RATING and then flee well away from this region by hurrying to 26.*

## 84

As you row nearer and nearer to the middle chasm, there is no doubt about the cause of those howling echoes. No longer can you convince yourself that it's just a trick of the wind. They are screeches and wails from deep within the trio of chasms and the whole island seems to shudder with them. Heaven knows what hideous beasts are their source. You try to shut your ears off to the terrifying sound as you steer your boat through the last line of jutting rocks and land it on the narrow shingle beach just in front of the middle chasm. Do you now choose to:

| | |
|---|---|
| Rest a while on the beach | **go to 43** |
| Explore the beach | **go to 285** |
| Approach the chasm immediately | **go to 122** |

## 85

You decide that your best means of escape is to hurry back to the chasm's entrance. So you splash through the swirling and fast-rising water, knowing that if you once lose your footing on the slippery rocks then you will almost certainly be dragged under by the vicious current. But you reach the outside again without mishap. You're just wondering whether you should use your rowing-boat to try and cross the whirlpool when the swelling sound from inside the chasm suddenly changes to a loud sucking sound. The whirlpool is disappearing again! *Go to 279.*

## 86

The head on the right expires first, sagging on to the creature's chest. The one on the left still gasps, though, its ape-like mouth distorted in agony. You're just about to give it a mercy blow when it, too, expires and the whole creature collapses on to the ground. You now move over to the vacated tomb, searching through the debris of decay inside with your sword. At last it spears a small gold crown, studded with diamonds.

*Add 1 to the score on your **TREASURE COUNTER**. Now hurry well away from this region by going to 136.*

### 87

As soon as you withdraw your hand from the nest, the grotesque bird flies off, wheeling back down into the chasm again. It's then that you notice a second nest a few metres further along the rocky ledge, also just within reach. And this nest also contains a precious egg. While the egg is only silver this time, the silver is studded with precious stones; rubies, emeralds and diamonds. But as before, there is a monstrous guardian to overcome first. You are carefully reaching down for the egg when another bird appears. This one is more like a gigantic eagle, with piercing, evil eyes and a beak as vicious as any sword. The most frightening feature of all, though, is its outspread wings – not feathers but flaming red fire.

>    If you wish to fight creature      **go to 199**
>    If you wish to avoid it            **go to 50**

### 88

The wizard starts to shake with apprehension, desperately trying to raise his dead eyelids. You see slits of motionless, yellowed white. 'Who are you?' he screams uncontrollably. 'You are not my trusty manservant. Who are you that tries to trespass into my cave?' You try to explain to him that you mean him no harm, that you came as a friend, but he suddenly seizes a bottle from a shelf in his cave, tearing it from the clinging cobwebs. He smashes it at your feet. A noxious green vapour rises and your mind becomes yet more confused and hazy. 'I might be blind and frail,' the demented wizard screeches at you, 'but I have the means to protect myself against murdering thieves such as you. Your strength will now be even less!'

***Deduct 1 from your STRENGTH RATING. Go next to 145.***

### 89

The misty face immediately wafts to one side, allowing you to enter the ice cavern, and its beautiful features rapidly disintegrate. Soon all that is left of them is a wispy chill. You tread with great care as you now step inside the cavern. Its glacial floor is treacherous and you have only soft leather boots on your feet. But you *do* have your trusty sword and so you decide to use this as a pick, thrusting it into the ice as you walk. ***Go to 147.***

### 90

To your immense relief, the punt-pole is suddenly thrust towards you and you exhaustedly grab it, allowing the goblin to pull you towards the raft. As you haul yourself on board, you feel half inclined to toss the nasty little creature into the swamp – but you let the temptation pass. 'I shall only transport you to the twelfth stepping-stone,' he tells you after he has retrieved your sword and shield from the swamp, 'then I must return to the bank.' Rather coyly, he adds, 'It's not every tenth stone but every *eleventh* that you must avoid. They're the real traps. So beware of your path across the swamp.' **Go to 49.**

### 91

The monstrous bird lets out a piercing squawk after your third sword thrust, shedding its feathers of fire all round you. You protect your head with your shield, waiting beneath it for the creature to drop. At last it does so, plunging like a stone into the chasm below. When its trails of smoke have cleared you return to the nest, reaching down for your much-deserved prize. '*Another defeat for you, Cragcliff!*' you cry defiantly into the chasm's vaults.

**Add 1 to the score on your TREASURE COUNTER. Now hurry well away from this region by going to 50.**

### 92

Walking round the left side of the temple, you suddenly slip on the icy ground just as you pass between two deep pits in the ice. Fortunately, however, you just manage to avoid these. But then you realise that you were not so fortunate. You dropped your shield when you slipped and it has disappeared down one of these pitch-black holes. You are not even sure *which* hole. As you peer down at the pits, you are amazed to hear a voice rise from them. **Go to 178.**

## 93

You again find yourself following a tunnel and, again, it brings you to a series of steps. This time the steps lead not up but down. At the bottom there are *two* tunnels, a short distance apart. Both appear to run in exactly the same direction but you wonder whether one might be more dangerous than the other. You peer into each to see if you can detect any traps inside, but both tunnels are pitch-black.

*If you have acquired INFRA-RED POWER during your adventure, you may employ it here to see through the darkness of the tunnels. Place the INFRA-RED POWER CARD exactly over the 'tunnel entrances' below. If you haven't acquired INFRA-RED POWER, you'll have to hope for the best in choosing which tunnel to follow.*

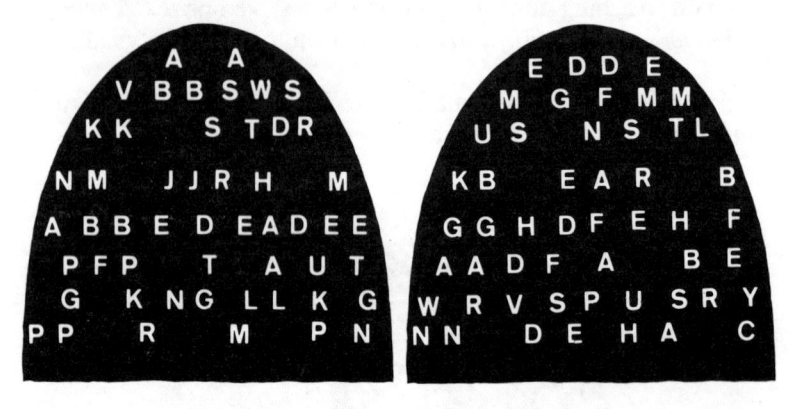

| | |
|---|---|
| If you prefer tunnel on left | **go to 220** |
| If you prefer tunnel on right | **go to 9** |

## 94

The gnome's dagger still pressed to your side, you start to chew the piece you have torn from the mushroom. It tastes quite good and so you hope that you have chosen the correct one. You certainly can't feel any adverse effects yet. But a few seconds later a strange withering sensation runs through your body. As you stagger to your feet the gnome starts to snigger again, his cave echoing with the horrible sound. You manage to make your way out of his cave and scramble down the rocks to the bottom of the cavern again. But you wonder how much longer you can last in this weakened state.

*Deduct 1 from your STRENGTH RATING. Go next to 148.*

## 95
## THIS CREATURE
## IS SLAIN BY

◇ 2 ◇

### WOUNDS

*Wage combat by simultaneously throwing the two dice. If you slay the creature, go to 239. If the creature inflicts a wound on you first, deduct 1 from your STRENGTH RATING and then flee well away from this region by hurrying to 136.*

### 96

The invisible hand releases you as you move towards the well on the right. The mysterious stranger is gone. You start to wind up the bucket but it seems to take an age before there is any evidence of it. At last you hear a faint clattering as the bucket slowly works its way up to the surface, knocking against the well's sides. As soon as you can reach it, you scoop out some of the stagnant water and trickle it over your head, just as you had been instructed. But your feeling of weakness remains. You must have chosen the wrong well. *Go to 157.*

### 97

The chiselled inscription reads: *Here lie the bodies of all those warriors who have failed in their quest against these caves. Each is buried with a treasure as a tribute to his endeavour. If the tombs be opened, the warriors will rise as monsters.* Far from being deterred by this inscription, you are keen to investigate the tombs. But which row of caves should you climb up to?

| | |
|---|---|
| If you prefer bottom row | **go to 59** |
| If you prefer middle row | **go to 203** |
| If you prefer top row | **go to 248** |

### 98

The creature keels over, collapsing on to the sand arena. It thrashes about weakly for a few moments and then is still for ever. The dwarf is aghast at your victory and, a bad loser, quickly yanks the sapphire ring from his finger. He pops it into his mouth, intending to swallow it, but then he sees your threatening approach with upraised sword. The terrified wretch spits the ring out into his hand and meekly offers it to you.

*Add 1 to the score on your TREASURE COUNTER. Now hurry well away from this region by going to 26.*

## 99

Fearing that the strange ball of mist might be poisonous, you cover your mouth until it passes. This happens very quickly and you are pleased to find that there are no apparent ill effects from the occurrence. Or are there? The water seems to be dragging you more and more. Eventually, though, you realise that it's not the water becoming stronger, it's you losing strength!

***Deduct 1 from your STRENGTH RATING. Go next to 293.***

## 100

Clambering up the rope on the right, you haul yourself into the hole just in time. A moment later the mountain of water comes crashing through your part of the tunnel. But then you find yourself up against a very different danger. The small chamber you have scrambled into is full of screeching bats. They are the size of crows and come skimming past your face, fangs gleaming in the dark. It's not their fangs that they use to overpower you, however, it's their stench. The foul smell they emit is quite appalling, curdling the air. You desperately clasp a hand to your mouth but it has little effect. With your head swimming from their nauseous secretions, you very soon collapse.

***Deduct 1 from your STRENGTH RATING. Go next to 306.***

## 101

Leaving the hag's cave, you find three more empty niches, each with water silently running down inside. Beyond them you notice another niche at a slightly higher level and you scramble up the steep wall of rock to investigate. At first you judge this one to be empty as well, for it's very small and cramped and seems to contain nothing but darkness, but then a floating face gradually appears out of the shadows. *Go to 204.*


## 102

As you open the chest on the right, a bat flies out at you and clings to your hand. It is much smaller than those bats that attacked you a few moments ago but it has claws of iron. You desperately try to shake it off but the claws sink deeper and deeper. It's only when you start to cry out from the unbearable pain that the urchin calls it off you with a high-pitched whistle. His concern is not for you, though, but himself. He's obviously worried that your cries might attract the attention of any nearby food-hunters. You now leave the cave feeling full of contempt for the wretch. But as you slide back down the rope into the tunnel, your arms feel weak and heavy. The bat must have injected some sort of poison into your hand. You only hope that it's not deadly.

*Deduct 1 from your STRENGTH RATING. Go next to 330.*

## 103

Ape-like, the grotesque creature squats in a small, damp niche to your right, baring its pointed teeth at you. Its slit-eyes are narrow, its nostrils hideously flared. There's a hefty sword at its side and the creature begins to drool saliva at the prospect of using it. You could easily flee this monster and continue further into the caves – its legs are stunted and clumsy – but it suddenly holds up a large, glinting diamond to the flickering torch to tempt you. Will you risk combat with it . . . or will you quickly pass it by, hoping to find a more easily attainable treasure further on?

| If you wish to fight creature | **go to 71** |
| If you wish to avoid it | **go to 278** |

## 104

Opening the chest on the right, you find a tiny chip of stone inside. 'That's to show that you have chosen correctly,' the little mason shouts across at you. 'That little stone was the very first piece I chipped away when I was chiselling out the chasm. It is my good luck charm. I hope the fact that you have found it will bring good luck to you, too. I offer my humble apologies for not trusting you.' ***Go to 20.***

### 105

Startled by the two sudden puffs of smoke, you are even more amazed when a head appears in each one. Both heads are of leathery, wrinkled skin and completely hairless. They each have penetrating eyes and a high collar rising up behind them. You guess from these high, important-looking collars that they are sorcerers. 'Yes, your assumption is right,' says the head in the puff of red smoke, reading your mind. 'We *are* both sorcerers.' ***Go to 208.***

### 106

You wearily reach the other side of the swamp at last and you rest a while at its edge. You're surprised to see that the goblin is still with you. Is he the good one or the evil one, though? – you still find it impossible to tell. There's a very faint kindness, however, in its otherwise unpleasant eyes and so you assume – hope – that it's the former. 'Do not leave the edge of the swamp just yet,' he tells you. 'There are four monsters that dwell in its depths. Two carry swords set with a diamond, two carry swords set with a ruby. If you wish to summon up the first pair, yell out Cragcliff's name once. If you wish to summon up the second pair, yell it twice. I must go now. Good luck in your combat.'

| | |
|---|---|
| If you decide to yell once | **go to 314** |
| If you decide to yell twice | **go to 44** |

## 107
## THIS CREATURE
## IS SLAIN BY

⟨8⟩

## WOUNDS

*Wage combat by simultaneously throwing the two dice. If you slay the creature, go to 258. If the creature inflicts a wound on you first, deduct 1 from your STRENGTH RATING and then flee well away from this region by hurrying to 324.*

## 108
Only seconds after you have climbed up into the hole, the bloodhounds appear beneath you. Suddenly losing your scent trail, they sniff around in confusion. You only hope that their handler, a huge brute of a man, doesn't look up and spot your hiding-place. You are at least thankful that you remembered to pull in the rope. To your relief, the handler eventually turns the bloodhounds round with a vicious yank on their leashes. 'Dumb beasts!' you hear him curse at them as they all disappear the direction they had come. 'I told you there wasn't anyone down this tunnel!' ***Go to 70.***

## 109

Exit from the Cave of the Stone Guardians is by yet another long, twisting tunnel. You wonder how much further it will be before you reach the very centre of the caves. Or perhaps you have already *passed* their centre – and you are now journeying towards the island's far side. But wherever you are, your progress through the caves is suddenly stopped by a heavy portcullis which drops down right in front of you. As you peer up into the darkness above to see where it came from, a voice starts to speak. 'If you wish the portcullis to rise,' the mysterious voice echoes, 'then you must speak the correct password. If you do not know it, then I will give you a chance to guess. Your choices are *Sillar*, *Phendon* or *Dradvil*.'

***If you have picked up the PASSWORD SCROLL during your adventure, you may consult it here to find out the correct password. If you haven't, you'll have to guess.***

| | |
|---|---|
| If you think it's SILLAR | **go to 272** |
| If you think it's PHENDON | **go to 303** |
| If you think it's DRADVIL | **go to 228** |

## 110

The tunnel is quite long – but there are no traps lurking in its darkness. And the air becomes warmer and warmer as you walk, making you soon forget the numbing cold of the ice cavern. Yes, you survived it . . . but you wonder what other hostile environments the caves have in store for you. Will this extreme cold be followed by extreme heat? Or will there be an even more extreme cold soon to follow, one that will test your stamina even more? ***Go to 325.***

## 111
## THIS CREATURE
## IS SLAIN BY

⟨8⟩

## WOUNDS

*Wage combat by simultaneously throwing the two dice. If you slay the creature, go to 268. If the creature inflicts a wound on your first, deduct 1 from your STRENGTH RATING and then flee well away from this region by hurrying to 54.*

### 112

'I am old Flint, the stone-mason,' the odd little man says, showing you his hammer and chisel as proof. 'It is I who constructed this chasm. It took me many, many years of patient chipping at the rock. As you can see, the only parts I didn't chip away are these two narrow crossings. I made one perfectly safe but the other such that it will collapse as soon as anyone steps on it. If you have a right to be in these caverns, then you will know which crossing you should choose. If you don't have that right, if you have come here as an enemy of Lord Cragcliff, then I shall enjoy watching you die!'

*If you have been taught the TRANCE SPELL during your adventure, you may cast it here to hypnotise the stone-mason into telling you which is the safest crossing. To do this, place the TRANCE SPELL CARD exactly over his 'mind square' below. If you haven't been taught the TRANCE SPELL, you'll have to hope for the best in making your decision.*

```
    S    R R   N      N O S

         L    T U R V      T
    J   O O E K K D     D      P

    K    U U F    T T    S      O
    N D I  B A A        H H     O

    O    N L G K T    N         M

    F T T    V    V H R    N
    S E     E    V  U   S    T
```

If you choose crossing on left     **go to 296**
If you choose crossing on right     **go to 22**

### 113

A revolting yellow gore oozing from the five places where you struck it, the creature drops to its fleshless knees. It tries to snarl its hatred at you but it's far too weak. It can't even give voice to its pain. There's now just a slight gasping from its throat. Rather than continue to watch this pathetic spectacle, you decide to search the tomb for its treasure. You do this with your sword, held at arm's length, because of the foul-smelling layer of decay at the bottom. You're not sure whether this is rotted embalming cloth . . . or flesh. Finally, your sword spears a loop of thick metal and you carefully lift it out. It's a solid gold armlet.

**Add 1 to the score on your TREASURE COUNTER. Now hurry well away from this region by going to 136.**

## 114

'Right, then let the parade of monsters begin,' the dwarf declares eagerly. Stumbling, he runs into the centre of the sand arena and hauls himself up on to a small rostrum. He picks up a whip lying there and cracks it in the air. 'First, let me present to you, Ugger,' he says, directing your attention to a large tunnel which emerges at the far side of the arena. A rusty portcullis slowly begins to raise there and out comes a snarling Neanderthal with a huge, bony head. A massive club dangles from its clumsy hand. 'As you can see,' the dwarf adds, grinning, 'not the most handsome of creatures. Nor the most intelligent. But very, very strong. If you wish to take little Ugger on, step into my arena.'

If you wish to fight creature **go to 83**
If you wish to avoid it **go to 275**

## 115

Opening the chest on the left, you find a small flask of liquid inside. You remove the stopper and down the potion in one. While you are waiting for it to take effect, the face in the water disappears. This rather concerns you. You're also concerned by the fact that the face was vaguely familiar. Whose was it? Yes, of course – it was that wizard again! Does this mean that the potion is another malevolence of his, that it is in fact *poison*? No, fortunately it doesn't because, far from expiring, you start to feel yourself gradually grow stronger.

***Add 1 to your STRENGTH RATING. Go next to 312.***

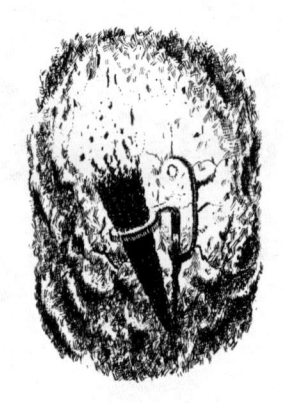

### 116

'You fool!' the urchin screams at you. 'That rock will now remain there for three whole months. Only then will it move itself back again.' You consider trying to lift the rock but the despondent creature tells you that its weight is even greater than it appears and the task would be hopeless. 'The only other way of leaving my cave,' he adds miserably, 'is by one of those two dark shafts in the back wall over there. I've never tried it myself because one of the shafts – I know not which – is cursed. But if you wish to risk it, that's your business. I shall just sit here and wait for those three months to pass.' Since you can't possibly sit around for that long yourself, you immediately start to investigate the two pitch-black shafts. Which will you crawl into?

***If you have acquired INFRA-RED POWER during your adventure, you may employ it here to see through the darkness of the shafts. To do this, place the INFRA-RED POWER***

***CARD** exactly over the two 'black entrances' below. If you haven't acquired **INFRA-RED POWER**, you'll have to hope for the best in making your decision.*

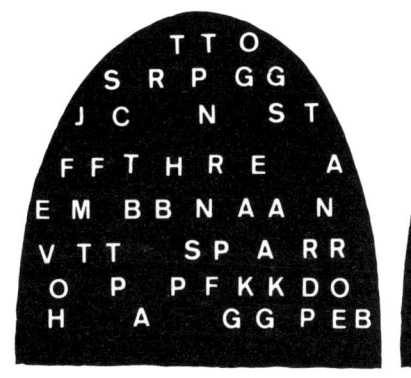

```
    T T O              D C C
  S R P G G          A U M M G H
 J C   N   S T      N N   S F T   A A
F F T H R E   A    D D A C   E E   H
E M B B N A A N    K H H K E M F F M
V T T   S P A R R  R N R   F H H   G I
O P   P F K K D O  U Q W   A   W R R
H   A     G G P E B H   A     N P E S
```

| If you choose shaft on left | **go to 19** |
|---|---|
| If you choose shaft on right | **go to 294** |

## 117
## THIS CREATURE
## IS SLAIN BY

⟨**9**⟩

### WOUNDS

*Wage combat by simultaneously throwing the two dice. If you slay the creature, go to 185. If the creature inflicts a wound on you first, deduct 1 from your **STRENGTH RATING** and then flee well away from this region by hurrying to 109.*

### 118

You just about manage to stagger to your feet, making your way as best you can beyond the tomb. The shaft of light becomes fainter and fainter behind you as you enter total darkness again. At a rough guess it took about two hundred paces to reach the centre of the pyramid and so you start counting out another two hundred paces. This should take you to its exit. When you do finally reach its exit, you find that like its entrance it consists of two dark arches. There is a torch flickering at the side of each arch but the light is only sufficient to penetrate the first couple of metres or so. Beyond that there is just pitch-darkness – hiding Heaven knows what dangers. Suddenly, a strange whisper echoes all around you. ***Go to 213.***

### 119

'You chose well,' the prophetess says as you drain the chalice on the left. 'If you had chosen the other, you would have been greatly weakened. If you had refused altogether the ice in this temple would immediately have turned to fire and we would all have been burnt alive. Now leave the temple by that door behind us. Good luck with your quest. We shall conduct a sacrifice in the hope that the gods may look favourably upon you.' ***Go to 74.***

### 120

The shaft of daylight rapidly grows bigger and brighter, and at last your boat emerges from the caves! You've survived those terrifying caverns! You cry out your joy to the vast open skies above, then start the long, arduous voyage back to Sageor's kingdom. The sea, too, seems to share your joy, for the waves and currents are much less hostile on this return crossing. You are soon within sight of Sageor's land . . . and of Sageor himself, still standing there on the cliff-top. Amazingly, it would appear that he had never deserted it. He must have had huge faith in your success. But how successful were you? To have survived Cragcliff's terrifying caves is one thing. To have defeated them, though, is yet another. Only if you can count at least six treasures in your haversack can you truly say that you have conquered the Caves of Fury . . .

***You have successfully reached the end of your adventure. If you think you could still improve upon your performance and collect even more treasures, however, try playing the game again.***

## 121

Slipping past the crab proved quite easy as its mobility was limited. It could only move from side to side, preventing it from making a fast turn. But you haven't progressed much further along the tunnel when you encounter another monstrous deposit of the tidal wave; a giant octopus! The huge, barnacle-encrusted tentacles undulate in every direction – surely as expert at suffocation as the

crab's pincers were at snapping a spine in two. But like the crab, this creature is not in its natural habitat – its movement along the dry floor of the tunnel is slow and cumbersome – and slipping past it would probably prove quite easy. Then you notice that one of those barnacles is, in fact, a large emerald . . .

> If you wish to fight creature **go to 195**
> If you wish to avoid it **go to 50**

## 122

You anxiously venture inside the gaping chasm and are greeted by a cacophony of distant echoing screams. Are these from tortured or torturer? Your blood runs cold but still you move forwards, deeper and deeper into the menacing shadows. Suddenly the screams stop and your heart pounds even faster as you guess that this silence is because the distant fiends are now aware of your arrival, curiously listening to your every step. Those steps, as soft as you try and make them, seem to be amplified into deafening thuds, the sound being carried right into the very depth of the chasm. *Go to 194.*

### 123

You hear the agonised scream more loudly as you are dragged along the tunnel by at least three pairs of muscular arms. The scream is very close now and you realise that you have been brought to some sort of terrible torture dungeon. There are evil-sounding cackles from your captors as your hands are forced above your head and fastened to a chain. A winch starts to creak nearby and you guess that you are about to be lifted off the ground. As you feel the excruciating wrench in your shoulders and arms your mind quickly starts to think . . . *Go to 24.*

### 124

It takes a huge amount of will power to resist sampling the water. Your throat feels like a desert and the gentle splashing of the drops at your feet must be the most tantalising sight you have ever seen. They look as clear as crystal. But you know that appearances can be deceptive and this harmless-looking trickle of water might be a trap set for you by Cragcliff. It might contain a deadly ingredient or one that seriously impairs your mind and body for the imminent quest. So you reluctantly move on, desperately wishing that you had brought your own fresh water supply. *Go to 194.*

## 125
## THIS CREATURE
## IS SLAIN BY

◇7◇

## WOUNDS

*Wage combat by simultaneously throwing the two dice. If you slay the creature, go to 261. If the creature inflicts a wound on you first, deduct 1 from your STRENGTH RATING and then flee well away from this region by hurrying to 136.*

## 126
Your mind dazed, your eyes blurred, you slowly come round. It takes you a while to realise what has happened. There was a sudden rock-fall, wasn't there? . . . you must have been knocked out. Fortunately, the fall has stopped now, the thick clouds of dust gradually settling. There's just the occasional trickle of gravel from above. But you still feel very weak, your movement stumbling and uncertain across the rubble. It's in this confused state that you hear a voice from the shadows ahead of you. *Go to 7.*

## 127
It is not much further before this branch of the stepping-stones joins up with the other two branches and the route becomes one again. As you wonder how much more there is to this swamp, you're sure you can hear light footsteps just behind you. You stealthily bring your hand to the hilt of your sword, suddenly swivelling round. It's that evil-faced goblin again! *Go to 81.*

## 128
The goblin winks at you as you decide to heed his warning, leaping clear over the tenth stepping-stone towards the eleventh. It's only

when you are in mid-air, and it is too late, that you realise what an evil wink it was. You were wrong to follow the goblin's advice – and you immediately find out why. The eleventh stone suddenly submerges before you reach it, leaving only the sluggish green slime before you. You're now about to find out just how deep it is. As you have feared, your feet fail to find the solid bottom – if there is one – and you desperately try to keep your head above the slurping mud. But the suction is tremendous and the effort quickly drains you of all your strength.

***Deduct 1 from your STRENGTH RATING. Go next to 53.***

### 129

Passing along the narrow walkway to the next cave, you again find that the effigy on the tomb is of the slain warrior that lies inside. But, if you touch this effigy, will it again turn into a monster that you would have to fight? You apprehensively run your finger along the stone warrior to find out. To your disappointment, it remains just as it is. But then the lifeless stone suddenly begins to change into a hog-faced fiend. A fanged, snarling mouth under evil slit-eyes.

Spiked armour-plating develops all over its humanoid body, and a horrific-looking mace sprouts in its hand. Dare you open the tomb to bring this fearsome creature to life?

> If you wish to fight creature   **go to 291**
> If you wish to avoid it   **go to 231**

### 130

The cook doesn't appear to notice which book you have picked up, returning to his spit. 'Another helping?' he asks amiably, drawing his razor-sharp knife the length of the carcass. While he is thus engaged, you stealthily try to open the book, but you have to shut it again quickly as the cook turns round. Seeing the knife glint in his hand, you drop the book into your haversack. It's only some twenty minutes later, when you have left the cave and have journeyed quite a way further along the tunnel, that you feel it's safe to examine the book properly. With agonised disappointment, you discover that it is merely one of the cook's recipe books. *Go to 93.*

### 131

The gnome leads you to the left wall of the cavern where there are three doors set in its thick ice. Each has an exquisite design of vines and birds carved in its centre. 'The alchemist lives behind one of these doors,' the gnome tells you. 'For him to invite you in he must hear you knock on the correct door. If you knock on one of the others first he won't trust you. He will assume you have come to steal his gold. I wish I could advise you which is the alchemist's door but my memory is poor and I can no longer remember.'

*If you have picked up the BOOK OF WISDOM during your adventure, you may consult it here to find out which is the right door. If not, you'll have to hope for the best in making your decision.*

> If you choose left door   **go to 236**
> If you choose centre door   **go to 262**
> If you choose right door   **go to 151**

## 132

You reach the other side of the arch without mishap. No pit suddenly opens up and no spears suddenly rain down. Nor do the rough walls of the arch move towards each other in an attempt to crush you. But how many of these terrors might have occurred if you had chosen one of the other two arches? It's a thought that makes you shudder so you immediately dismiss it from your mind, just thankful that you have passed through the entrance in one piece. ***Go to 58.***

## 133

You're just about to reach into the tomb to lift out the treasure when a terrifying roar comes from the darkness at the far end of the cave. It's a two-headed demon; the heads reptilian but the muscular body human. You let the lid of the tomb fall so you can draw your sword.

But, as the heavy stone crashes back into place, the demon suddenly vanishes again. It obviously only materialises when the lid of the tomb is raised. So, if you wanted, you could quite safely leave this cave and go to investigate the next one. But what about that exquisite gold chalice? Even though it means making that abominable creature reappear, you're very tempted to raise the tomb's lid a second time . . .

>    If you wish to fight creature    **go to 259**
>    If you wish to avoid it    **go to 287**

## 134

You have followed this branch of the stepping-stones for some distance when you suddenly notice that the fourth stone ahead of you has a strange yellow glow. You wonder if this means that it has been touched with magic and you curiously step towards it. But then you wonder what *type* of magic – good or bad? Perhaps the glow causes anyone setting foot on the stone to be turned to stone themselves. So, do you step on this stone or take the precaution of leaping right over it to the next one?

>    If you wish to step on stone    **go to 341**
>    If you wish to leap over it    **go to 127**

## 135

Feeling rather dubious, you duck your head to enter the gnome's cave, then notice two huge mushrooms growing in its centre. The gnome sniggers, his hunched shoulders quivering within his shabby cloak. 'They are all the food I ever require,' he explains proudly. 'As soon as I've devoured them, they grow again. Now you must partake as well.' Not fully trusting the gnome, you decline his offer, but then he suddenly produces a small dagger from the folds of his cloak. You reach for your sword but there's not enough space in the cramped cave for you to draw it out. The gnome jumps at you like a cat, pressing the dagger to your side. He has you in his power. ***Go to 205.***

## 136

Glad to be able to put the eerie catacombs behind you, you soon find yourself at an underground river. There's a rowing-boat moored there and you wonder whether you should take it. Could this underground river possibly lead back to the open sea? 'Yes, I can tell you that it does,' confirms a voice behind you, somehow able to read your thoughts. You turn round to find a small wizard standing there, dressed in a long green gown. ***Go to 265.***

### 137

Strangely, the river soon becomes gentle once more, with only the slightest of currents. You allow your boat to drift for a while so you can recover a little from your strenuous exertions. As you are resting, you suddenly notice three small chests squeezed into the front of the boat. You lean forward to examine them, wondering if they might contain some of the wizard's magic potions. They each have the same design carved into their lids; of flowers and nymphs. ***Go to 65.***

### 138

As you put the mysterious cave further and further behind you, your hunger pangs intensify. You're now very much regretting that you didn't take the risk of investigating it. Your concern is not just about the satisfaction of your appetite but also of a more serious nature as your increasing hunger is likely to have an effect on your strength. So you decide to make the long trek back towards the cave. When you at last reach it, however, you find that the opening has been completely filled in by a rock-fall. All that extra walking was for nothing . . . and now you feel weaker than ever.

***Deduct 1 from your STRENGTH RATING. Go next to 93.***

**139**

You are just about to enter the ice cavern when the frozen wisps in front of you gather into the vague outlines of a female face. You think you can see a mouth there and a pair of haunting, beautiful eyes. 'I am Crystalor, guardian of the ice cavern,' the mouth says, speaking slowly. 'If you wish to pass through it, then you must offer the correct password. I can give you three choices – but only one chance. Your choices are *Dradvil, Cherlin* and *Torzad*.'

*If you have picked up the PASSWORD SCROLL during your adventure, you may consult it here to find out the correct password. If not, you'll have to hope for the best in making your decision.*

If you choose DRADVIL **go to 232**
If you choose CHERLIN **go to 27**
If you choose TORZAD **go to 89**

**140**

'Watch!' the Chief Sorcerer commands. 'You shall now glimpse the face of your enemy.' His features now slowly depart from the blue mist, which then gradually changes from blue to black. There's an evil mocking laugh from within the mist and with some trepidation you prepare for Cragcliff's features to start appearing there. But then the mist suddenly changes to a dazzling white, temporarily blinding you. Realising that your guess at the password must have been wrong, you anxiously wait for your sight to return. Fortunately, it does – but you now feel sick and dizzy.

*Deduct 1 from your STRENGTH RATING. Go next to 15.*

## 141
## THIS CREATURE IS SLAIN BY

⟨8⟩

## WOUNDS

*Wage combat by simultaneously throwing the two dice. If you slay the creature, go to 193. If the creature inflicts a wound on you first, deduct 1 from your STRENGTH RATING and then flee well away from this region by hurrying to 45.*

## 142
You have followed the middle branch of the tunnel for quite a way when you suddenly hear the echo of stamping feet. It's coming from behind you – and it's getting louder and louder. You draw out your sword but then you realise that there's more than just the one pair of feet in that fast-approaching sound. There must be at least twenty. Guessing that this is a whole unit of Cragcliff's warriors – far more than you can handle – you desperately search for somewhere to hide. *Go to 38.*

## 143
As light as the steps of your leather boots are, the massive cavern seems to boom with the echo of them as you cautiously walk down its centre. It's not long before you arrive at a small pyramid, built of rough lumps of the reddish rock. There are two arched entrances into this pyramid, both uneven and dark with sinister shadows. Fearful that one of these might spring a trap as soon as you step inside, you wonder which you should choose.

*If you have acquired INFRA-RED POWER during your adventure, you may employ it here to see through the darkness and find out which entrance is safest. Place the INFRA-RED*

***POWER CARD** exactly over the two 'black arches' below. If you haven't acquired **INFRA-RED POWER**, you will have to hope for the best in making your choice.*

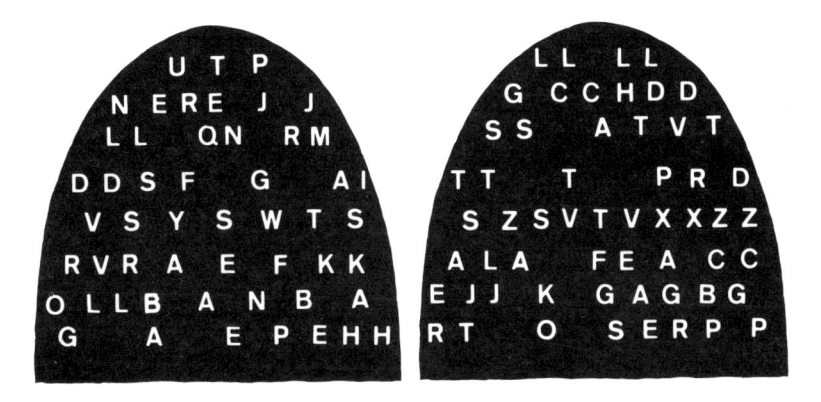

If you choose entrance on left     **go to 311**
If you choose entrance on right     **go to 60**

### 144

No sooner have you plunged into the well in the centre than the water loses its warmth. In fact, it immediately starts to turn to ice, solidifying all about you. It was a treacherous lure! As it creaks and splinters, the ice taking more and more of a hold, your breaths become shivering gasps. You try to reach for the edge of the well but the ice has you ensnared. You can't move. But you must if you're not to become forever frozen in that ice – for you are sure that is the well's intention – and you make one last desperate effort. Not knowing how, you at last find yourself out of the deadly well. But you have been severely weakened by that numbing cold.

***Deduct 1 from your STRENGTH RATING. Go next to 334.***

### 145

You cautiously continue along this tunnel, finding it growing narrower again. At last you join up again with what appear to be the other two branches and the tunnel suddenly becomes wider. It's now a long, continuous cavern, with large, dripping caves to either side. In some the drips have created thick stalactites reaching right to the ground, forming cage-like lines of bars across the caves. And suddenly, you see a fanged, muscular brute inside one cage, pounding its huge fists on the stone bars. If the gaps between the stalactites are too narrow for the brute, though, they are not too narrow for you. Taking a deep breath, you could just about squeeze into its cage. But why in the name of the gods should you want to? Because the blood-stained sword at its belt has a hilt of pure gold . . .

| If you wish to fight creature | **go to 40** |
|---|---|
| If you wish to avoid it | **go to 304** |

### 146

You suddenly feel a splash of water in your face. 'You don't die yet, dog!' you hear as you come round. 'We want to prolong your suffering as much as possible!' But the brute approaches just a bit too close and, summoning up every last grain of strength, you suddenly swing your legs towards him. You wrap your thighs round his neck, squeezing harder and harder until the brute cries out to his assistant to operate the winch again and lower you down. As soon as your arms are free, you wrap one of these round his neck instead, threatening to throttle him if any of the others come near. You're dragging him towards the dungeon's exit as a hostage when one of the other prisoners dangling from the wall calls out to you. ***Go to 266.***

### 147

As you carefully wander through the gleaming ice cavern, a soft chanting sound reaches your ears. It seems to be coming from a temple before you. This is no ordinary temple, though, because although it has a domed roof and fluted pillars, it is constructed wholly of ice. Its door is of ice and so are the two statues on either side of this door. The door is partly open and you wonder whether you should enter it. Perhaps it would be wiser, though, to pass to one side of the temple.

| If you wish to enter temple | **go to 329** |
| If you wish to pass to left | **go to 92** |
| If you wish to pass to right | **go to 284** |

### 148

You haven't gone much further round the right side of the cavern when you come across a small rock-pool. It's the stillest pool you've ever seen, its surface like glass. Not one drip of water shimmers it, not one slight breeze. As you kneel down, wondering whether you

might drink at it, you see your reflection as sharply as if in a polished mirror. To your amazement, it suddenly starts to speak to you. 'This is the Pool of Reflections,' it says calmly. 'You now cannot leave this pool until I allow you to leave it. For me to do this, you must speak the correct password. What is it? When you speak it, then I will speak it too. But this will not necessarily mean you have chosen correctly. I am, remember, but reflection.'

*If you have picked up the PASSWORD SCROLL during your adventure, consult it here to find out the correct password. If you haven't, you'll have to hope for the best in making your choice.*

| If you think it's PHENDON | **go to 270** |
| If you think it's SILLAR | **go to 61** |
| If you think it's DRADVIL | **go to 224** |

### 149
### THIS CREATURE IS SLAIN BY

⟨2⟩

### WOUNDS

*Wage combat by simultaneously throwing the two dice. If you slay the creature, go to 173. If the creature inflicts a wound on you first, deduct 1 from your STRENGTH RATING and then flee well away from this region by hurrying to 54.*

### 150

There's just a slight hissing from that elongated tongue as the odious creature lies dying on its side. It stares at you with powerless hate in its eyes as you now use your sword to poke around inside the tomb. There's a foul-smelling layer of decay in there but you bravely stick to your task, eventually spearing a thick gold armlet. It is studded with diamonds and rubies. You turn round to torment the loathsome creature with your find but its eyes are now closed and its tongue finally silent.

*Add 1 to the score on your TREASURE COUNTER. Now hurry well away from this region by going to 136.*

### 151

You notice the goblin scurry away as you rap on the right-hand door a couple of times. When there's no answer, you try again, knocking even louder this time. *Still* there's no answer and so you assume you must have chosen the wrong door. Since the goblin is no longer there to watch you, you decide to slip across to the door in the centre. You don't knock at this one but quietly turn the handle in case it isn't locked. You're in luck – it isn't! But that's as far as your luck goes because the cave behind it is completely empty. So it must be the door on the left that is the alchemist's. You quietly move across to this one as well but just as you're about to turn the handle, the wood suddenly changes to thick iron. And you hear at least a dozen bolts simultaneously sliding across behind it. You couldn't force the door open now, even with a battering-ram! ***Go to 74.***

## 152

The creature makes one last lash at you, tearing furiously at the empty air as it sinks to the ground. You step over its now still body, making your way to that glinting diamond in the far corner of the cage. It's as large as your fist – and with not a single flaw.

***Add 1 to the score on your TREASURE COUNTER. Now hurry well away from this region by going to 324.***

## 153

'So it's as I thought,' the dwarf accuses you from his rostrum, pointing a stunted finger at you, 'you're a chicken-liver! But don't think that was the last of my monsters. There's one more my whip commands!' Your eyes return to the portcullis, waiting for it to raise again. It remains firmly closed, however, and you wonder what the dwarf can mean. You find out at the next crack of his whip – and what you see makes you step back in horror. No sooner has the whip

hissed through the air than the dwarf starts to grow. It is slow at first, but bigger and bigger he gets, soon becoming even taller than yourself. He retains his dwarfish appearance with his large head and stunted limbs, but those features now turn green and hideously wart-ridden and his whip starts to sprout deadly iron spikes.

If you wish to fight creature **go to 48**
If you wish to avoid it **go to 26**

### 154
You'd been expecting terrifying roars and howls from the creature as it received your final blow. But it dies in complete silence. There's just the clank as its heavy sword drops from its limp hand. The creature then slumps to its knees and quietly lays itself down. Almost pitying it, you force yourself to be philosophical. If you hadn't killed it, it would have killed you. And how much pity would *you* have been shown? So you step over the creature, returning to the tomb. You now push the heavy lid right off and hook out the chalice with the tip of your sword.

*Add 1 to the score on your TREASURE COUNTER. Now hurry well away from this region by going to 136.*

### 155
As you rest weakly at the edge of the pool, your reflection reappears. You are angry at it after what it has done but this anger isn't mirrored back at you. The expression in the water remains perfectly calm. 'Just as I have reduced your strength,' it speaks softly, 'I can restore it. There are two white pebbles near where you are sitting, one to your left and one to your right. Toss one of these into the water. If you toss the correct one, then you will regain all the strength you have lost here. But which is the correct pebble? Make your choice with care – because you cannot try the other one afterwards.'

*If you have been taught the TRANCE SPELL during your adventure, you may cast it here to hypnotise your reflection into telling you which is the right pebble. To do this, place the*

***TRANCE SPELL CARD** exactly over its 'mind square' below. If you haven't been taught the **TRANCE SPELL**, you'll have to hope for the best in making your decision.*

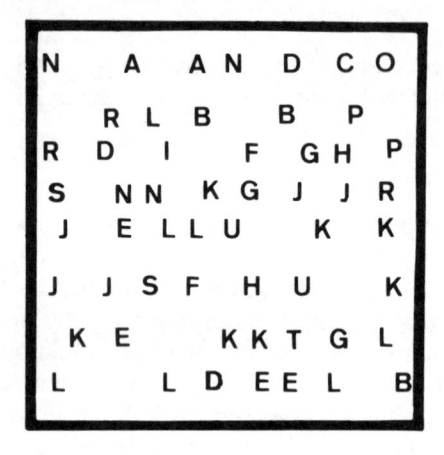

```
N    A    A N    D    C  O
     R L  B      B    P
R    D    I      F    G H   P
S    N N  K G    J    J     R
 J   E    L L U       K     K

J    J  S F     H    U      K
 K  E           K K  T  G   L
L         L   D  E E  L     B
```

If you choose pebble to your left     **go to 313**
If you choose pebble to your right    **go to 11**

### 156

You wipe your brow with an exhausted arm as the creature's writhing finally stops. It twitches no more – it's dead. But an evil-smelling gore still spills from its wounds, sticky, green and foamy. So you act quickly in prising the emerald from its breast-plate, manipulating the tip of your sword at arm's length. When the jewel is free, you draw it towards you along the ground, keeping your other hand across your mouth. The stench is so bad that you decide not to examine your treasure until you are well away from this battle site. When you have put it a good distance behind you, you hold up the emerald to the nearest torch flame. It's absolutely flawless! Smirking at your first victory over Cragcliff, you put your prize safely away in your haversack.

***Add 1 to the score on your TREASURE COUNTER. Now hurry well away from this region by going to 45.***

## 157

When you finally leave the Hall of Mysteries, it's merely to find yourself entering another large cavern. This is not quite as massive as its predecessor but its echoes are still deep and hollow. The entrance to this cavern also has an inscription. Chiselled ornately into the rock are the words: *Cave of the Stone Guardians*. You soon see why it has acquired this name because you notice several stone statues amongst the shadows. Approaching the first of these statues, you see that it is of a hideous, squat monster with a thick, muscular body. It has a bony head with large fangs protruding

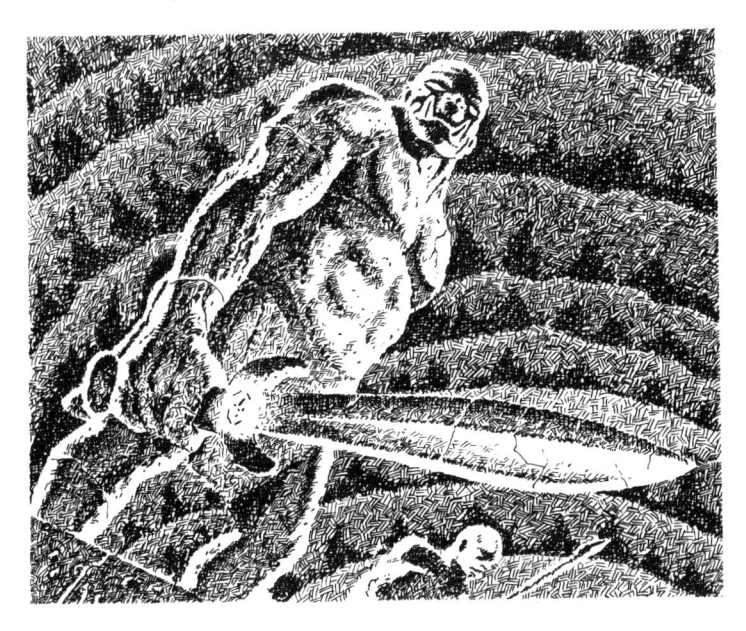

upwards from its lower jaw. But the effigy isn't completely repulsive. For set in the creature's stone sword is a large, flawless emerald. Your fingers are just about to examine this gem to see how easily it might be removed, when you notice a warning chiselled into the statue's plinth. It reads: *Beware! If any part of this statue be touched the creature will immediately come to life.*

If you wish to touch statue     **go to 223**
If you wish to avoid it     **go to 52**

## 158

You assume that your password must have been correct because the wizard allows you to step into the boat. As you row it away from him, however, his pointed fingers send a shaft of purple light at you. You start to see stars before your eyes and the world suddenly appears very strange to you. Your boat now seems to be approaching a huge waterfall, even though there isn't a waterfall there. But to you this waterfall is as real as can be and you frantically try and paddle away from it as it draws you towards its deadly edge. Your efforts are frenzied, rapidly sapping your strength. At last the wizard's spell begins to wear off and the imaginary waterfall disappears. Is it too late, though? For you now lie collapsed on the floor of the boat.

*Deduct 1 from your STRENGTH RATING. Go next to 137.*

## 159

Sure that this goblin is the same as the other – and even if he wasn't, who's to say that he doesn't possess equal malice? – you keep to the stepping-stones. You're rather concerned, though, that you don't hear his angry frustration behind you. There's not a single curse from him. You're just beginning to wonder whether he did have your welfare at heart after all when the stone you've just stepped on suddenly bursts into flames. You desperately jump to the next but that does the same, the flames over two metres high. *Go to 244.*

**160**

The slime gurgling higher and higher, you desperately tell the goblin that you are not a stranger but one of Cragcliff's bodyguards who has lost his way. The other's nasty features suddenly look alarmed. 'If that is true,' he says nervously, 'then I humbly beg our master's forgiveness. But how do I know that is true? If you are who you say you are then you should know the correct password for the swamp. What is it?'

*If you have picked up the PASSWORD SCROLL on your adventure, use it here to find out the correct password for the swamp. If you don't have the SCROLL, you'll have to guess it.*

> If you think it's KRAVIX     **go to 90**
> If you think it's GARLON    **go to 289**
> If you think it's RUTHLOR    **go to 218**

**161**
**THIS CREATURE**
**IS SLAIN BY**

◇ **9** ◇

**WOUNDS**

*Wage combat by simultaneously throwing the two dice. If you slay the creature, go to 315. If the creature inflicts a wound on you first, deduct 1 from your STRENGTH RATING and then flee well away from this region by hurrying to 50.*

**162**

As you paddle past the skeleton, it roars furiously at you from the bank. It was the huge axe in its hand that deterred you. The blade was thick with dried blood from the creature's previous battles. It obviously employed the weapon with immense skill. You hope that another creature will appear but it looks as if that was your one and only chance to challenge for the diamond. You are nearly out of the caves now, the shaft of daylight growing larger and larger in front of you. Suddenly, though, there's a terrifying roar from the opposite

bank. A snarling mercenary stands there; spiked armour all over its hideous ape-like body. His huge scimitar howls through the air as he tauntingly invites you to challenge him.

> If you wish to fight creature  **go to 32**
> If you wish to avoid it  **go to 67**

### 163

The invisible hand leads you forward, its fingers cool and gentle, eventually bringing you to three wells. Each has an ornate design of flowers and nymphs carved round its rim. 'If you are wise,' a mysterious voice whispers, 'you can restore your strength. If not, you will have to remain in this weakened state. One of these wells has a spring at the bottom that will cure your dizziness. All you have to do is winch up the bucket and trickle its contents over your head.

The other two wells also have a spring at the bottom but their curative powers, I'm afraid, are nil. So choose wisely – for only one attempt is allowed you at these wells.'

*If you have picked up the BOOK OF WISDOM in your adventure, you may consult it here to find out which of these wells is the right one. If you haven't acquired it, you'll have to hope for the best in making your decision.*

| | |
|---|---|
| If you choose left well | **go to 302** |
| If you choose centre well | **go to 181** |
| If you choose right well | **go to 96** |

### 164

You haven't explored very far along this left branch when you hear a slight rumbling sound from the darkness above. The rumbling quickly subsides, however, so you ignore it. But then it starts up again, growing much louder this time. The ground begins to vibrate under your feet, as do the rocky walls when you press a palm to them for support. It seems to be an earth tremor. You quickly press your whole body to the rough wall as fragments of stone come bouncing down from above. A moment later it's small rocks, then much larger ones. There are now boulders crashing down, filling the air with flying splinters and thick clouds of dust. The rocks have all miraculously fallen clear of you so far but then one ricochets towards your head, knocking you unconscious.

*Deduct 1 from your STRENGTH RATING. Go next to 126.*

## 165
## THIS CREATURE IS SLAIN BY

⟨6⟩

### WOUNDS

*Wage combat by simultaneously throwing the two dice. If you slay the creature, go to 98. If the creature inflicts a wound on you first, deduct 1 from your STRENGTH RATING and then flee well away from this region by hurrying to 26.*

### 166

You decide you can rest no longer and you painfully ease yourself up from the shingle and start to explore the damage done to your boat. The gash is quite wide but you manage to find a piece of driftwood that fits it perfectly. Giving it a few blows with a large stone, you wedge it into the gash, confident that this will hold long enough for you to make your journey back from the island. That's as long as you don't run aground on any more rocks. And as long as you *survive* the island, of course. Your heart freezes when you suddenly hear a hideous moan from the huge chasm just behind you, seeming to come from the depths of Hell itself. With hand tense on the hilt of your sword, you slowly venture inside the gaping chasm . . . ***Go to 300.***

## 167

But the discovery of the two dangling ropes seems too good to be true and you are suspicious that one of these pitch-black cavities might contain a trap of some sort. You'll have to make your choice between them very quickly, however. The crashing surge of water sounds as if it's about to reach you at any moment!

*If you have acquired INFRA-RED POWER during your adventure, you may employ it here to find out which of the arch-shaped holes is safe. To do this, place the INFRA-RED POWER CARD exactly over each of the two 'black arches' below. If you haven't acquired INFRA-RED POWER, you will have to hope for the best in making your choice.*

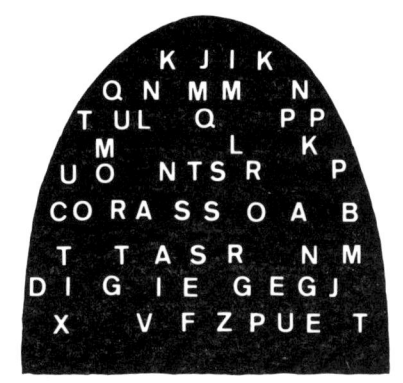

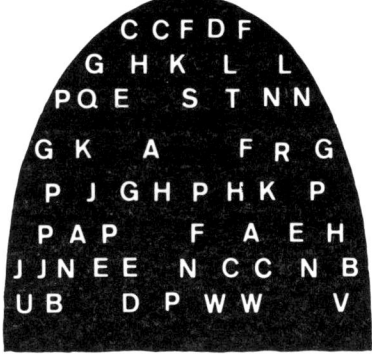

If you decide on left hole     **go to 298**
If you decide on right hole     **go to 100**

## 168

The wizard immediately swings round to confront you, his long white beard swishing through the air. 'Ah, I should have just used my eyes, shouldn't I?' he growls at you, those eyes piercing in their aged sockets. 'Why did I waste our time with passwords? It's quite obvious that you're not the novice I was expecting! Who are you? What is your name?' Although the old man is nothing to fear physically, bent and frail as he is, you are concerned about the magic powers he might have at his disposal and so you try to placate him. You tell him that you intend him no harm but he chooses to ignore you. Then his pointed fingers suddenly send a streak of violet light towards your chest. It's like a bolt of lightning, sapping your strength.

*Deduct 1 from your STRENGTH RATING. Go next to 145.*

### 169
### THIS CREATURE
### IS SLAIN BY

◇ 8 ◇

### WOUNDS

*Wage combat by simultaneously throwing the two dice. If you slay the creature, go to 323. If the creature inflicts a wound on you first, deduct 1 from your STRENGTH RATING and then flee well away from this region by rowing to 120.*

### 170

As soon as you utter your guess at the password, the hooded apparition divides, becoming mere mist again, parting a way for you on to the bridge. When you reach the top of the bridge, however, the stone suddenly begins to crumble. You desperately run for the far end but the whole thing collapses before you make it. You fall with the crumbling rocks into the swamp below. The next thing you know you are lying on the first of the stepping-stones at the far side of the bridge. You must have been concussed by one of the rocks but luckily washed up on to this stone – or were you so lucky? Your gently probing fingers discover a deep gash at the back of your head.

*Deduct 1 from your STRENGTH RATING. Go next to 49.*

## 171

You have travelled some distance along this branch of the stepping-stones when you notice an inscription at your feet. It has been gouged into the stone, although some of the letters have been worn almost flat with age. You can just about read: *It was one of the other two branches that you should have chosen, Adventurer. You would have been given a magical power there. But now it is far too late. You cannot turn back.* Glancing round, you find out just why you can't turn back to one of the other two branches. Every single stepping-stone behind you has suddenly vanished. ***Go to 127.***

## 172

Being careful not to kick the rope into the pit, thereby allowing the skeleton to escape, you step round the dark crater. You start following the torch-lit tunnel again but it's not long before you hear the scrape of iron against rock to your left. There's a low, throaty cackle from the shadows and then a reptile-headed dwarf suddenly appears before you. Its long, forked tongue whips out from a leathery mouth, lashing to left and right. Again, this is a creature you could outpace if you chose but your eyes are entranced by the sparkling emerald at the centre of its breast-plate. The creature sees your temptation . . . and cackles again, preparing its sword.

| If you wish to fight creature | **go to 211** |
| If you prefer to avoid it | **go to 45** |

### 173

Just as you had hoped, the swamp-creature's webbed fingers make for a rather awkward grip on its sword. You're able to get in your lethal thrusts quite easily. It drops its weapon as, screaming and whining with pain, it retreats into the deeper parts of the swamp to die. You quickly rescue the sword before it is lost in the slime and carry it back to firm ground so you can prise out the huge diamond from its hilt.

*Add 1 to the score on your TREASURE COUNTER. Now hurry well away from this region by going to 54.*

### 174

The urchin starts to explain his test. 'One of the two chests which you *didn't* choose is completely empty,' he says. 'The other one contains a trap. If you can pick the correct chest a second time I will know that you can be trusted.' So you once more look down on the two chests, anxiously glancing from one to the other.

*If you have been taught the TRANCE SPELL during your adventure, you may cast it here to hypnotise the urchin into telling you which is the correct chest. To do this, place the TRANCE SPELL CARD exactly over the urchin's 'mind square' below. If you haven't been taught the TRANCE SPELL, you'll have to hope for the best in making your decision.*

```
        P   A   C   A   B   H
        R   E K   C       I
    K   L   I S       S S   J
    N M     H U G     U     K
    O   L   E G       D D   O
    S   R B E   B H D       P
    U   Q       M   F N     Q
    W       S A T B Y Y     T
```

If you choose left chest     **go to 230**
If you choose right chest    **go to 102**

### 175

You feel the rim of a goblet of water at your lips, then fumbling, fat fingers tug your hood right off. 'How can you ever forgive us, master?' a concerned, ugly, stubbled face implores you. 'We didn't realise . . .' it stammers on as your feet are lowered to the floor, 'we deserve the same punishment ourselves!' When your hands have been freed, you make it appear that you're about to order a punishment even *worse* than that, causing your three captors to cower at your feet. While they are grovelling there, you swiftly and silently make your escape from the dungeon. ***Go to 93.***

## 176
## THIS CREATURE IS SLAIN BY

⟨2⟩

## WOUNDS

*Wage combat by simultaneously throwing the two dice. If you slay the creature, go to 152. If the creature inflicts a wound on you first, deduct 1 from your STRENGTH RATING and then flee well away from this region by hurrying to 324.*

## 177

The creature staggers as you deliver the fatal thrust of your sword then becomes one with the swamp again as it sinks slowly into oblivion. A slight gurgling of the mud, a few viscous green bubbles, are all that's left of it. No, there is *also* its sword. You suddenly spot it just about to submerge some distance from its owner. The defiant creature must have flung it away just to spite you when it knew its end had arrived. But you manage to wade to the heavy weapon before it is eternally lost under all the slime. You carry it back to dry land so you can remove the ruby from its hilt.

***Add 1 to the score on your TREASURE COUNTER. Now hurry well away from this region by going to 54.***

## 178

'Your shield is at the bottom of *both* these dark pits,' the mysterious voice tells you. 'I see that you are greatly puzzled by this,' it adds with a booming, mocking laugh. 'You only dropped one shield but I speak of two. Ah well, that is one of the mysteries of the ice cavern! In one pit your shield is of iron still but in the other it is merely of wood. Which pit will you choose to climb into? Your climb will be easy but your choice is not so. You may descend into only one of these pits and the shield you find there is the one you must keep.'

*If you have acquired INFRA-RED POWER during your adventure, you may employ it here to see through the darkness of the pits. To do this, place the INFRA-RED POWER CARD exactly over the two 'black holes' below. If you haven't acquired INFRA-RED POWER, you will have to hope for the best in making your choice.*

```
      N E E                          V G  E
    D G  F  H                      N U T T  N
  N E C   I P   E R              L W V    W      Z M
P E W  I       L      M        I S T   O F I EN      O
 K M K L N R M F   F            K  B  C   A A C D B H
 K U T  O    P O R L            L  B C R B O      D E K
  T  H O  K N L N T              S R Q  P  N L  M  L  F
 N E   V V   U T U D   N        R Y    W  O V U T N    D
```

If you choose left pit    **go to 196**
If you choose right pit    **go to 23**

## 179

If this is the wrong arch, you are sure that if you make a dash through it you can easily avoid any danger that might be waiting for you. The other end looks only a couple of seconds away if you run.

But as soon as you enter the arch, a spear flicks out from either side, piercing the flesh of your upper arms. Fortunately, your path was right through the centre of the arch and so neither wound is very deep. But you anxiously wonder whether those spears had been tipped with poison.

***Deduct 1 from your STRENGTH RATING. Go next to 58.***

### 180

The creature screams and howls its rage at you as you remain at the edge of the swamp. It obviously can't walk on firm ground and needs you to wade into the swamp to join it. Finally, though, its enraged taunts subside and it retreats whence it had come, into the deeper part of the swamp. Scarcely has its grotesque head submerged than another swamp creature surfaces, squelching towards you. This looks not unlike the first but its body is squatter and its feet are webbed, not its hands. It raises one of these feet right up from the clinging slime as it now enters the shallow edge of the swamp. You see the leathery webs between the three stumpy toes and you guess that this second creature will be even more reluctant to venture on to firm ground than the first. Again, it's you who will have to wade into the swamp.

If you wish to fight creature **go to 79**
If you wish to avoid it **go to 54**

### 181

As you move towards the well in the middle, you suddenly feel the cool hand release you. The invisible stranger is gone. Praying that you choose correctly, you now start to hoist up the bucket. It seems to take an eternity before you hear a faint clattering far below. It's the bucket knocking against the sides of the well as it slowly works its way up to the surface. As soon as you can just reach the bucket, you scoop out some of the water inside and let it trickle over your head as you were instructed. Your feeling of weakness remains, though. Your choice was obviously wrong. *Go to 157.*

### 182
### THIS CREATURE
### IS SLAIN BY

⟨**6**⟩

### WOUNDS

*Wage combat by simultaneously throwing the two dice. If you slay the creature, go to 150. If the creature inflicts a wound on you first, deduct 1 from your STRENGTH RATING and then flee well away from this region by hurrying to 136.*

### 183

You're just beginning to think that you chose correctly when the tomb suddenly creaks open. A bandaged arm reaches out from it, reeking of decay. You grab for your sword but the arm is too quick for you, its yellowed fingers taking you by the throat. Its strength is ten times that of any human grip and you cough and splutter as it lifts you off the ground. The hand squeezes tighter and tighter and you feel yourself passing out. When you finally come round, the tomb is closed again, an innocent hush hovering over it once more. But you're not sure if you have the strength even to stand up, severely weakened as you are by that near strangulation.

*Deduct 1 from your STRENGTH RATING. Go next to 118.*

### 184

'You won't chance your luck with my demon either,' the dwarf observes, cracking his whip once more. He's now taunting you, as if he suspects you of cowardice. 'Well, if you don't like hot, perhaps you will like cold. Enter my ice dragon!' A burst of splintering ice precedes this next monster, the freezing blast it causes reaching

even to your side of the large arena. You shiver . . . then shiver again as you now behold the source of this icy flare. It is both beautiful and horrific, a dragon shimmering from head to tail with a delicate blue frost but also sporting lethally sharp icicles. These deadly spikes dangle menacingly from its jaws.

> If you wish to fight creature **go to 219**
> If you wish to avoid it **go to 153**

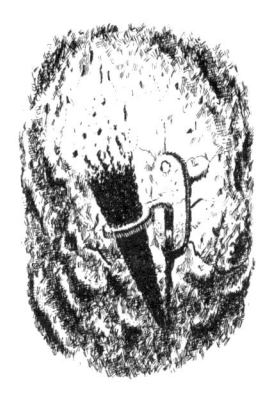

### 185

The creature lets out a blood-curdling shriek from the depths of its cloak as it sinks to the ground. Its shark-like teeth still gnash fiercely as you stand over it but then its jaws finally come to rest. The moment it does, the vanquished creature immediately turns to stone again. You search for a large, pointed rock and use this to chip the ruby away from the statue. At last you free it. You briefly hold the ruby up to one of the flickering torches to admire its beauty before putting it in your haversack.

***Add 1 to the score on your TREASURE COUNTER. Now hurry well away from this region by going to 109.***

### 186

Taking a deep breath and clenching your teeth, you force up the portcullis with all your strength. It creaks and raises a little – but not enough for you to slip underneath. So you have another go, your arm muscles feeling as if they are about to explode from the massive strain. At last you raise the iron monstrosity just high enough, but as you slowly squeeze through to the other side, you wonder whether you have done yourself serious damage. You feel as if you're about to collapse from the terrible exertion.

***Deduct 1 from your STRENGTH RATING. Go next to 66.***

### 187
### THIS CREATURE
### IS SLAIN BY

### ⟨9⟩

### WOUNDS

***Wage combat by simultaneously throwing the two dice. If you slay the creature, go to 98. If the creature inflicts a wound on you first, deduct 1 from your STRENGTH RATING and then flee well away from this region by hurrying to 26.***

### 188

You haul yourself up into the hole in the roof just in time. A minute later the unit of warriors comes running through the tunnel. You peep out at them from your hiding-place. Your calculation was right – there are at least twenty of them. They are grunting chants as they run and you guess that they are on a training exercise. It looks absolutely gruelling, perspiration dripping from their bodies. But those bodies are huge, they are built like oxen, and you are glad that you took this evasive action. You could probably have taken a couple of them on, even three, but you would surely have been no match for the whole unit. ***Go to 33.***

### 189

You had assumed from what the wizard told you that the rest of your journey through the caves would be straightforward. You'd hoped it was just a matter of letting your boat *drift* to the outside.

But as you're lying back in the small craft, resting from all your adventures, you see that the river splits into three branches ahead. Each branch disappears into an arched tunnel. As you come nearer to these arches, each with an intricate carving of nymphs and flowers above it, you wonder which you should steer towards.

*If you have picked up the BOOK OF WISDOM during your adventure, you may consult it here to find out which is the right arch. If not, you'll have to hope for the best in making your decision.*

| | |
|---|---|
| If you choose left arch | **go to 307** |
| If you choose centre arch | **go to 340** |
| If you choose right arch | **go to 35** |

### 190

Unfortunately, the chest you chose is empty. But there is *some* good news for you. The tidal wave underneath has now passed, mysteriously leaving the tunnel almost completely dry once again. So you start to climb back down the rope, bidding farewell to the urchin. You can't really bear him a grudge over the bats, given the great fear he must constantly be living in. 'I wish your breed well,' you tell him as he retreats nervously into the shadows behind the hole. 'I hope that they will one day be a thriving race again, free from all persecution.' ***Go to 330.***

## 191

The final statue you come to is of a cloaked creature. It is the most human-looking of the three although its hands are more like claws, with curling fingernails. But the face is devoid of all flesh and the teeth are like knives, pointed for death, the eyes eerily grey and lifeless. Once again, this statue has an inscription beneath it, warning one not to touch. Therefore, again there must be a reason for wanting to touch it and you search for that reason. Ah, there it is! – a large ruby deep within the folds of the cloak.

If you wish to fight creature **go to 117**
If you wish to avoid it **go to 109**

## 192

For the first twenty steps you think it possible that you have chosen the correct stairway. During the next twenty you become doubtful. After that, as you grow more and more tired from the exhausting climb, you realise with despair that you must have chosen wrongly. The stone steps seem to go on and on, climbing higher and higher through the rock, but still there's no sign that you are about to reach the top of the chasm again. As the inscription warned, this dark stairway is much longer than it should be. Still the steps don't end, twisting round and round, higher and higher. At last, though, you spot some light way, way above you. This must be the top – but do you have enough strength left in your exhausted body to make it?

*Deduct 1 from your STRENGTH RATING. Go next to 20.*

### 193

As the skeleton writhes its last, you pick up its spiked helmet which fell from its head during the last stages of the combat. Using the tip of your sword, you prise out the dazzling ruby and put it into your haversack. With a triumphant grin, you then haul yourself out of the pit, climbing the rope to the path at the top.

*Add 1 to the score on your TREASURE COUNTER. Now hurry well away from this region by going to 45.*

### 194

The huge cavern gradually narrows as you grope your way deeper and deeper into it, eventually becoming no more than a large tunnel. It soon merges with two other tunnels which you assume lead from those other chasm entrances you saw. You're continually expecting the shadows on either side suddenly to move and a monstrous creature to leap out at you. But Cragcliff doesn't play completely unfair with his challengers. A series of flickering torches fastened to the rocky walls now leads the way onwards. It's in the dim light of one of these torches that you suddenly spot your very first fiend . . . *Go to 103.*

## 195
## THIS CREATURE IS SLAIN BY

⟨8⟩

## WOUNDS

*Wage combat by simultaneously throwing the two dice. If you slay the creature, go to 331. If the creature inflicts a wound on you first, deduct 1 from your STRENGTH RATING and then flee well away from this region by hurrying to 50.*

## 196

The pit is not nearly as deep as you were expecting; only three or four metres. Its darkness is deceptive. Reaching the bottom, you immediately start to feel round for your shield. As soon as you have found it, you anxiously test its weight, praying it's still made of iron. But no, its lightness tells you it has become wood. Cursing your luck, you haul yourself out of the pit again by a series of handholds dug into the ice. Now that you are able to see your shield in the light, you realise that it could still be of some service to you. It is made of a very hard wood – teak or mahogany. All the same, you can't pretend that this substitute hasn't left you considerably weaker than you were before.

*Deduct 1 from your STRENGTH RATING. Go next to 245.*

**197**

The creature lets its spiked club fall to the ground so it has both hands free to clasp its wounds. It throws back its head in pain, its fanged mouth emitting an agonised howl. The whole cave seems to shudder with the terrifying cry. Finally, though, it subsides and the creature crashes to the ground. As soon as its claw-like hand has stopped writhing, you relieve it of its three precious bracelets. It doesn't seem right, anyway, for workmanship of such beauty to adorn a thing so hideous.

*Add 1 to the score on your TREASURE COUNTER. Now hurry well away from this region by going to 136.*

**198**

For a moment you wonder whether the gigantic dwarf has in fact been slain. Its prostrate body, still at first, suddenly starts to have life again. You prepare to strike it once more – but then you realise that its movement is simply a shrinking of its body. It is returning to the diminutive size it was before. In fact, it shrinks even further than that, ending up no larger than a small rabbit. The sapphire ring rolls from its tiny, shrivelled finger, wobbling to rest in the sand. After wiping it clean, you drop your fairly-won prize into your haversack.

*Add 1 to the score on your TREASURE COUNTER. Now hurry well away from this region by going to 26.*

## 199
## THIS CREATURE IS SLAIN BY

⟨3⟩

### WOUNDS

*Wage combat by simultaneously throwing the two dice. If you slay the creature, go to 91. If the creature inflicts a wound on you first, deduct 1 from your STRENGTH RATING and then flee well away from this region by hurrying to 50.*

## 200

Removing your sword, you immediately plunge into the well on the left. But you are soon wishing that you had kept it with you for the water strangely drags you down until your head is submerged. A layer of ice then quickly forms across the surface, trapping you underneath. If you had had your sword with you, its weight might have pulled you down even further, but you would have had something with which to break the ice. As it is, you have only your bare hands – and they prove quite useless. You can hold your breath no longer and as you start to take helpless gulps of the icy water you are sure your end has come. Suddenly the layer of ice cracks open and you rise gasping and spluttering to the surface. But do you still have enough strength left to heave yourself out of the numbing water?

*Deduct 1 from your STRENGTH RATING. Go next to 334.*

## 201

Careful not to miss your footing on each of the shadowy steps, you eventually reach another tunnel much higher up. You realise how deep you must have burrowed into the caves because you still seem to be far from the island's surface. The higher-level tunnel is just as dark and cold, the echoes just as muffled. It's in one of these echoes that you think you suddenly detect a scream of pain. You warily move along the tunnel to investigate but then a hood is thrown across your eyes from the shadows behind. Before you can draw your sword, your hands are securely manacled behind your back. ***Go to 123.***

## 202

'You may take the boat,' the wizard tells you slowly. He says it rather strangely but you assume this is because he's disappointed that you guessed the password. You know how annoyed wizards can sometimes become when others match their cleverness. As you row away from him down the river, you at first find the task very easy. The river has a slight current and it's going with you. But then the current suddenly seems to switch direction, becoming stronger and stronger. Soon you feel you are rowing against a huge rapid, each pull on the oars wrenching at your arms. The muscles of your face now clenched to distortion, sweat pouring from your brow, you wonder how much more you can take . . .

***Deduct 1 from your STRENGTH RATING. Go next to 137.***

**203**

When you have climbed the steps to the middle row of caves, you follow the narrow walkway that leads from one eerie entrance to the next. You slowly venture inside the first of these caves, your breathing so tense and heavy that it nearly extinguishes the candle in there. The flame flickers precariously for a moment before you quickly shield your mouth. The warrior's tomb lies quiet and still in the centre of the cave and you anxiously approach it. Bracing yourself, you raise the heavy stone lid, opening it a crack. You peer into the tomb. When you observe what is inside, however, you immediately drop the lid again. You saw a cloaked skeleton, with only the evil glint of a pair of eyes visible under its hood. The rest of

the face appeared to be just a black void. But you also saw the gleam of a magnificent diamond pendant on the skeleton's chest . . . and you wonder whether to lift the lid of the tomb again. That would mean, of course, having to fight the grotesque monster.

        If you wish to fight creature    **go to 125**
        If you wish to avoid it    **go to 255**

**204**

Its features are of blue mist; wise ancient eyes under a deep, lined brow. Hair flows wildly at the temples and chin. 'I am Mentor, the Chief Sorcerer of the Hall of Mysteries,' his slow whispering voice announces. 'I can show you the face of your mortal enemy, Cragcliff. But first you must tell me the correct password.'

*If you have picked up the PASSWORD SCROLL during your adventure, you may use it here to find out the correct password. If you haven't, you'll have to hope for the best in making your choice.*

| | |
|---|---|
| If you think it's PHENDON | **go to 222** |
| If you think it's SILLAR | **go to 273** |
| If you think it's GARLON | **go to 140** |

**205**

'I said you must partake of the mushrooms as well,' he insists. 'You've already guessed, of course, that one is not really a mushroom at all but a poisonous toadstool. The genuine mushroom is the one on the left. No, I mean the one on the right.' He starts to snigger again with delight. 'Left . . . right. Left . . . right. I'm not going to tell you. You'll just have to decide for yourself!'

*If you have been taught the TRANCE SPELL during your*

*adventure, you may cast it here to hypnotise the gnome into telling you which really is the harmless mushroom. To do this, place the TRANCE SPELL CARD exactly over the gnome's 'mind square' below. If you haven't been taught the TRANCE SPELL, you'll have to hope for the best in making your decision.*

```
        D   A E E    A      J   D
            L   M M R K     E
        N O D O K R    T N G
          A  P E   L   S    S F
        A       T   T  I   R R   J
          B    V V   F     T T
        S    C  O  P    U G     L
        D S S    P    P H   R M
        E     M  Q T P M    T
```

If you wish to eat mushroom
    on left                          **go to 94**
If you wish to eat mushroom
    on right                         **go to 221**

### 206

Still trying to gauge the depth of the swamp, wondering whether it might be possible to wade through it, you suddenly notice a series of stepping-stones some fifty metres to your left. They lead towards the middle of the swamp – and, you assume, through the hanging mists right to the other side. So you hurry towards the start of these stones, testing your weight on the first one's flat surface. The stone doesn't even wobble, so you start crossing from one to the next. You've only reached the ninth stone, however, just about to stride out to the tenth, when a high-pitched voice suddenly shrieks at you from behind. ***Go to 10.***

## 207

You continue to let your boat drift down the river as the grotesque manic laughter gradually fades. You keep glancing from one bank to the other, anxiously wondering when the creature will make its appearance. Suddenly, there's a blood-curdling cry from your left and an armoured skeleton steps out of the shadows. It brandishes a huge battleaxe at you, challenging you to row towards the bank and

fight it. Again, that hideous laughter starts to vibrate through the caves. 'Well . . . will you try your hand against it or not?' the mocking voice demands. 'This might not be your only chance to win that diamond from me. There might be more creatures to come. But how many times dare you risk letting a chance go?'

| | |
|---|---|
| If you wish to fight creature | **go to 78** |
| If you wish to avoid it | **go to 162** |

## 208

The green sorcerer suddenly breaks into an unsettling laugh. 'Yes, your assumption was right,' he echoes the other. 'We *are* both sorcerers. But can you also guess which one of us is here to do you evil? Is it me – or my red friend over there? My instruction to you is to pass to the left of the tomb . . . ' Now the red one breaks into a cackling laugh. 'And mine,' he says, 'is to pass to its right!'

*If you have been taught the TRANCE SPELL during your adventure, you may cast it here to hypnotise the two sorcerers into telling you which advice is best. To do this, place the TRANCE SPELL CARD exactly over their joint 'mind square' below. If you haven't been taught the TRANCE SPELL, you'll have to hope for the best in making your decision.*

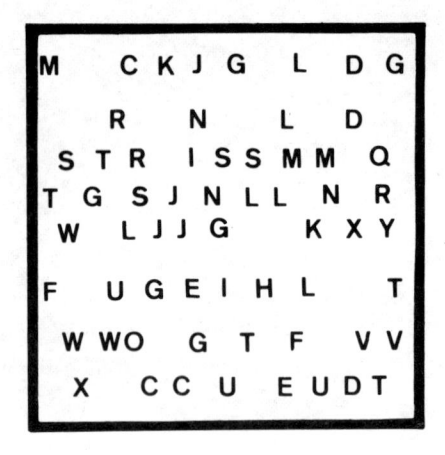

```
M     C K J G    L   D G
    R    N     L   D
  S T R   I S S M M   Q
T G S J N L L   N   R
W   L J J G       K X Y

F   U G E I H L         T

  W WO   G  T  F    V V
    X   C C  U   E U D T
```

| If you decide to pass on left side | **go to 14** |
| If you decide to pass on right side | **go to 321** |

### 209

You choose the left chasm as the cove there looks an easier one for landing your rowing-boat, not quite as rocky as the other two. But it's the chasm furthest away from you and so it means at least half a mile extra rowing. The task is much more strenuous now because of the fierce currents created by the island's proximity. It seems constantly to draw you towards its treacherous rocks. As strong as your arm muscles are, you start to feel them tire as you have to dig deeper and deeper into the heavy water. It's like heaving against thick mud. You finally reach the furthest chasm, rowing up on to the narrow shingle beach there, your body in a state of complete exhaustion.

*Deduct 1 from your STRENGTH RATING. Go next to 41.*

### 210

'Come, follow us,' one of the maidens invites you. 'We are maidservants of the cooling cave and we will show you where the plunge pools are so you can refresh yourself.' They lead you through breezes quite heavenly after all that stifling heat – fresh and deliciously scented. The large cavern is green with delicate, hanging vegetation; grapevines and exotic tendrils. Fine waterfalls tumble amongst the greenery and harp music echoes gently in every niche. It is to one of these niches that the maidens take you, and you find yourself staring into the clearest rock-pool you have ever beheld. You are left to relax in this pool and you review your good fortune as you do so. If you hadn't guessed the correct password and been able to take immediate relief from that heat, you might not have had enough strength to continue your quest.

*Add 1 to your STRENGTH RATING. Now that you are revived go to 145.*

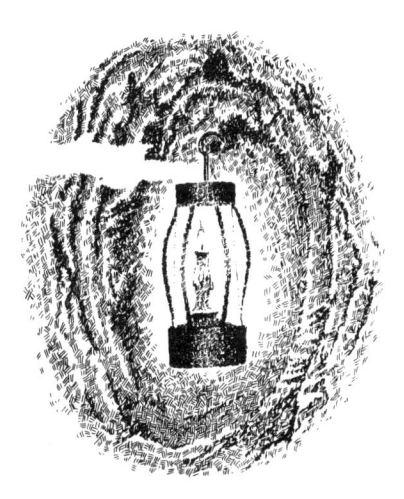

## 211
## THIS CREATURE IS SLAIN BY

⟨2⟩

## WOUNDS

*Wage combat by simultaneously throwing the two dice. If you slay the creature, go to 156. If the creature inflicts a wound on you first, deduct 1 from your STRENGTH RATING and then flee well away from this region by hurrying to 45.*

## 212

'Your password is wrong.' The hooded apparition speaks quietly, its voice no more than a whispering breeze. 'You must turn back.' Of course, having ventured this far you can't even consider turning back and so you reluctantly draw your sword. 'You know that weapon of yours can't help you against me,' the figure murmurs calmly. 'I am not flesh and blood like other creatures you may encounter here. I am mere mist. You can pass through me with ease but if you do the risk is yours.' But what risk can there possibly be? you suddenly ask yourself. Mist is just mist. So you step right up to the floating figure and then slip through it to the rise of the bridge. It's only as you reach the other side, joining the stepping-stones again, that you feel much of your strength suddenly drain away.

*Deduct 1 from your STRENGTH RATING. Go next to 49.*

## 213

'Do not fear these exits,' the mysterious whisper tells you. 'They are not like the entrances, one hiding a trap. They are both perfectly safe. But you should still choose with care which exit you leave by. For while one will do you no harm, the other will benefit you. There is a pitcher of aromatic oil hidden in one of these arches.

Smear this over you and it will restore the strength the mummy sapped from you. So I say again – choose with care.'

*If you have acquired **INFRA-RED POWER** during your adventure, you may employ it here. Place the **INFRA-RED POWER CARD** exactly over the two 'dark exits' below. If you haven't acquired **INFRA-RED POWER**, you will have to hope for the best in making your choice.*

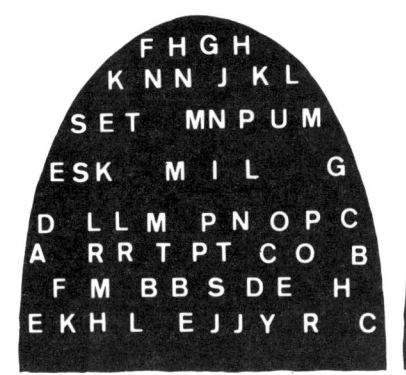

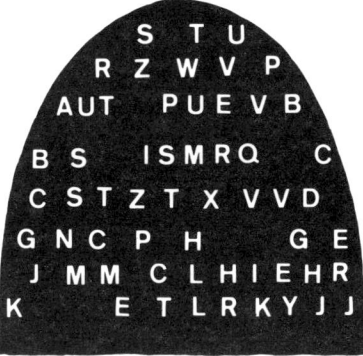

If you choose left exit    **go to 292**
If you choose right exit    **go to 62**

## 214

As soon as you have emptied the goblet, you feel a strange tingling in your body. Your aching muscles suddenly start to feel alive again, the acute pain in them disappearing. You soon feel you have regained all your strength. Indebted to that other prisoner, you quickly look round for more of the liquid so he can benefit from it as well. But the poor wretch tells you to leave the dungeon at once, before more of the torturers arrive. 'For me it's too late,' he murmurs. 'I am so far gone that no amount of the liquid can save me. But I shall take final comfort in the fact that I have helped another escape. Now hurry, be off – while there's still time!'

***Add 1 to your STRENGTH RATING. Go next to 93.***

### 215

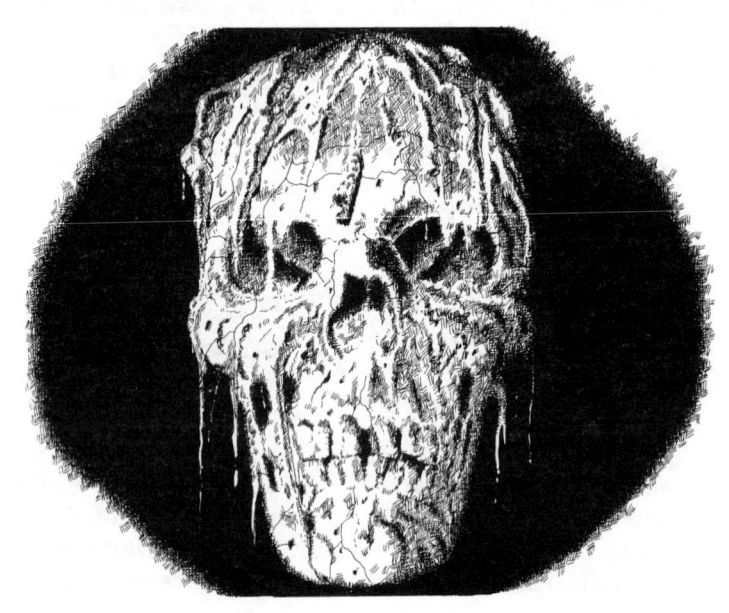

The creature bellows furiously at you, spitting mud and slime, as you decide to wait for its partner. It attempts to come up on to the dry land after you but its stunted legs are obviously adapted only for the swamp. Tottering precariously, it finally gives up and, furious, it makes its way back to the depths of the mist-shrouded swamp. As the huge mud bubbles it leaves on the surface finally disappear, another creature suddenly erupts from a different part of the swamp. This one is a decomposing corpse and it's difficult to tell whether the green tatters hanging from its bones are tangles of slime or rotting flesh. Its teeth are set in bony jaws, all its skull cavities empty. In fact, the only part of this grotesque apparition not to revolt the eye is the dazzling ruby in its sword. The grinning creature taunts you with this jewel, a skeletal finger inviting you into the swamp to join it.

> If you wish to fight creature    **go to 111**
> If you wish to avoid it    **go to 54**

### 216

Bowing your head slightly to enter the cave, you can now just discern a slight flickering glow at the far end. The flickering becomes a little brighter as you approach it and you realise it is an orange-flamed fire crackling away in a nook. Above the fire is a spit with a smoking animal carcass and tending this spit is a benign-faced cook. He is stripped down to the waist because of all the heat and his muscular body glistens in the light of the leaping flames. You remain just beyond the light of the fire so he cannot see your face. 'Ah, is that one of Cragcliff's bodyguards come for his sustenance?' he enquires, peering into the darkness. 'Sit yourself at that table there and I will slice you off a leg. It's just about ready.' ***Go to 82.***

### 217

You notice an inscription above the arches which reads: *These are entrances to two stone stairways leading back to the top of the chasm. One is much shorter than it should be and will weaken you no more than you already have been. The other is ten times as long as it should be and may even be the end of you. Choose with care. Once you have started you cannot turn back.*

**If you have acquired INFRA-RED POWER during your adventure, you may employ it here to see through the darkness of the holes and work out which stairway is the shortest. To do this, place the INFRA-RED POWER CARD exactly over the two 'black entrances' below. If you haven't acquired INFRA-RED POWER, you will have to hope for the best in making your choice.**

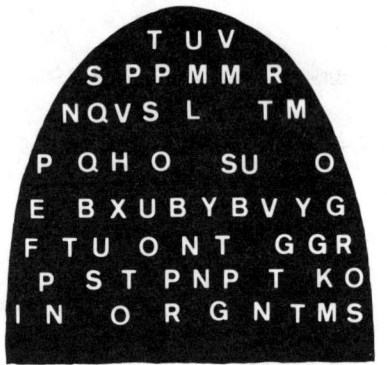

| If you choose left arch | **go to 192** |
|---|---|
| If you choose right arch | **go to 68** |

### 218

It seems that your guess at the password was correct because the goblin jabs the end of his punt-pole towards you again and this time he doesn't suddenly yank it back. But just as you're about to seize hold of the pole, he cracks it down hard on your head. He viciously swipes the pole at you again but you quickly raise one of your arms from the slime, grabbing hold of it. The goblin desperately tries to shake you off but you work your hands up the long pole, finally reaching the raft. There's a terrified scream as, with one blow, you knock the evil little creature into the gurgling slime. But you have no opportunity to gloat over the way it quickly swallows him up. For that first crack on the head he gave you was a severe one and you suddenly slump to your knees.

***Deduct 1 from your STRENGTH RATING. Go next to 49.***

**219
THIS CREATURE
IS SLAIN BY**

⟨**9**⟩

**WOUNDS**

***Wage combat by simultaneously throwing the two dice. If you slay the creature, go to 308. If the creature inflicts a wound on you first, deduct 1 from your STRENGTH RATING and then flee well away from this region by hurrying to 26.***

**220**
Tentatively running your hand along the rough wall, you feel your way into the tunnel on the left. You haven't gone far when you feel something move round about your feet. At first, you assume it to be

a mouse or a rat – but then you realise that it's something much worse for you hear a quiet hissing sound. It's a snake – in fact, a whole writhing mass of them. You run deeper and deeper into the tunnel, hopping from side to side, in a desperate attempt to escape them. At last the hissing sound recedes behind you but you feel a strange throbbing in your calf which slowly spreads to the rest of your body. One of those snakes must have injected its venom into you. All you can do is hope that it's not deadly.

***Deduct 1 from your STRENGTH RATING. Go next to 318.***

### 221

You start to chew the piece you have torn from the mushroom, the gnome's dagger still pressed sharply to your side. You swallow – and wait. There's no adverse effect. The mushroom actually tastes quite good so you tear off some more. The gnome snarls at your impudence. 'Naargh – you think you're so clever, don't you?' he says through a mean, twisted mouth. 'I ought to make you taste some of the other mushroom as well – the poisonous one – but it's lucky for you that there's a penalty for me if I don't play fair. This good mushroom will no longer replenish itself and my food supply will be gone!' Just to spite the malicious gnome, before leaving his cave you defiantly tear off another large piece of his mushroom. ***Go to 148.***

### 222

'Watch!' the blue misty face commands. 'You shall now glimpse the countenance of your enemy.' The sorcerer's features gradually metamorphose in front of you, the eyes becoming darker and darker. They are now a glinting black, deep-set and fringed with a low unbroken brow. The mist is now like a thick soot, not just the eyes but the whole face dark with evil. The beard – as coal black as the eyes – suddenly rips open from side to side and a set of dazzling white teeth is revealed as the face broadens a grin at you. This grin now turns to a manic laugh . . . but you can watch no more. You turn away from the evil, mocking apparition before it freezes the courage in you. *Go to 157.*

### 223
### THIS CREATURE
### IS SLAIN BY

### ◇ 9 ◇

### WOUNDS

*Wage combat by simultaneously throwing the two dice. If you slay the creature, go to 17. If the creature inflicts a wound on you first, deduct 1 from your STRENGTH RATING and then flee well away from this region by hurrying to 109.*

### 224
After your reflection has mouthed the password with you, it again speaks independently of yourself. 'You will, I am sure, be thirsty after all your adventures,' it says. 'Drink some of this water to quench that thirst.' Assuming that you must have chosen the correct password and that this is your reward, you lower your face to the pool. The water tastes delicious, cool and fresh. But as you rise to your feet again, you start to stagger, almost toppling into the pool. That liquid obviously reduces one's strength. You can only hope it's nothing worse!

*Deduct 1 from your STRENGTH RATING. Go next to 155.*

### 225

You frantically try to swim against this approaching danger but suddenly you strike your head against one of the vicious protrusions and everything goes dark. When you come round you find yourself lying on the damp but drying floor of the chasm, the whirlpool having strangely disappeared again. Miraculously, you have no broken bones, the whirlpool has done your body no further harm. But you have an aching head and your fingers find blood when they feel the gash on it . . .

*Deduct 1 from your STRENGTH RATING. Go next to 194.*

### 226

Opening the centre chest, you find a tiny brass urn inside. 'You have chosen correctly,' the urchin tells you, his grubby features looking genuinely pleased for you. 'Drink the potion you will find inside the urn and it will make you feel as strong as you did before my bats attacked you.' Although the liquid looks very unappealing – muddy brown and frothy – you do as the urchin instructs and quickly swallow the potion. Immediately, your head starts to clear again . . .

*Add 1 to your STRENGTH RATING. Go next to 69.*

### 227
### THIS CREATURE
### IS SLAIN BY

$$\langle 9 \rangle$$

### WOUNDS

*Wage combat by simultaneously throwing the two dice. If you slay the creature, go to 277. If the creature inflicts a wound on you first, deduct 1 from your STRENGTH RATING and then flee well away from this region by hurrying to 50.*

## 228

There's an anxious wait for a few minutes while the portcullis remains exactly where it is. Then you hear the pulleys start to creak again way above you and the rusty iron slowly lifts from the ground. As soon as it is high enough, you slip underneath. Eagerly continuing your journey through the tunnel, you wonder what you would have done if your password *hadn't* been correct. You would surely have had no option but to turn round, your quest at an abrupt end. ***Go to 66.***

## 229

Fortunately, you notice two dangling ropes a short distance ahead of you, several metres apart. They each lead up to a sort of pothole in the roof of the cave and you decide to hide in one of these until the bloodhounds have passed. But could there be a trap in one of these holes? They are impossible to see into; quite pitch-black.

***If you have acquired INFRA-RED POWER during your adventure, you may employ it here to see through the darkness of the holes in the roof. To do this place the INFRA-RED***

***POWER CARD** exactly over their two 'black entrances' below. If you haven't acquired **INFRA-RED POWER**, you will have to hope for the best in making your choice.*

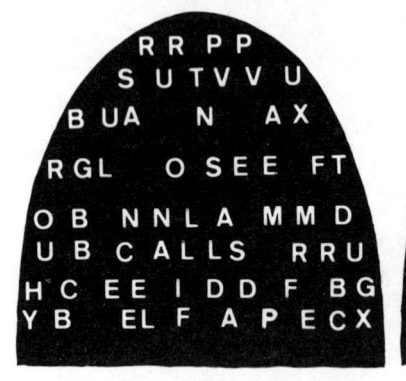

| If you choose hole on left | **go to 64** |
|---|---|
| If you choose hole on right | **go to 108** |

### 230

The urchin's grubby features once more reveal a slight smile. 'You chose correctly again,' he tells you. 'For the Fates to favour you twice you must indeed have only good in your heart. I'm sorry I had to be so suspicious. But us urchins can't be too careful or our breed will be completely wiped out.' After anxiously peering out of his hole to make sure the coast is clear for you underneath, the little creature shakes your hand and wishes you luck. When you reach the bottom of the rope, you briefly glance up to wave him goodbye. But he has already retreated nervously into the shadows of his hole. ***Go to 330.***

### 231

Exactly the same occurs at the next cave you come to. As soon as you touch the stone warrior lying on top of the tomb, it provides you with a hideous glimpse of the foe you can expect. This foe is two-headed; the head on the right a half-decayed skull and the one on the left even more grotesque, ape-like with a mouth crammed full of blood-dripping fangs. Fortunately, they have only the one weapon between them but this is a terrifying barbed sword. It's function is clearly not just to slice and cut but to saw and hack as well.

If you wish to fight creature    **go to 283**
If you wish to avoid it          **go to 322**

### 232

You assume you have given the correct password because the misty face wafts to one side to let you enter the cavern. Indeed, she even seems to give you her blessing because you feel her icy kiss on your cheek. But you soon realise that the kiss isn't as harmless as it first seemed. It lingers with you, turning colder and colder on your cheek. It now seems to be burning a hole into your flesh, sharp as an icicle. You can only hope that this kiss wound was just to weaken you a little . . . and not to finish you off altogether.

***Deduct 1 from your STRENGTH RATING. Go next to 147.***

## 233

Suddenly, one of the prophetesses addresses you, although her face remains downward. 'All who enter our temple must drink from one of these two chalices,' she says while the others continue to chant. 'One potion is harmless but the other will drain your strength. You may think it better to refuse altogether. But if you do refuse, you will die.'

*If you have been taught the TRANCE SPELL during your adventure, you may cast it here to hypnotise the prophetess into telling you which is the harmless chalice. To do this, place the TRANCE SPELL CARD exactly over her 'mind square' below. If you haven't been taught the TRANCE SPELL, you'll have to hope for the best in making your decision.*

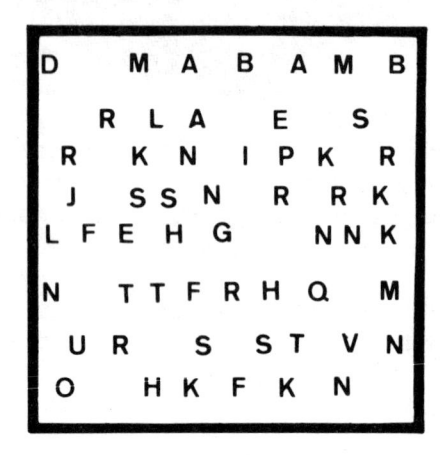

```
D   M  A  B   A  M   B
    R  L  A      E    S
R   K  N  I   P  K    R
J   S  S  N      R  R K
L F E  H  G         N N K
N      T  T  F  R  H Q   M
    U  R     S   S  T V  N
    O     H  K   F  K    N
```

| If you wish to choose chalice on left | **go to 119** |
|---|---|
| If you choose chalice on right | **go to 297** |

## 234

The creature drops squealing to the ground, rolling on to its back to die. The eyes are set in an eternal stare. Not wishing to look upon this chilling sight for a moment longer, you hurry across to the tomb again and reach inside for the diamond. Did those evil eyes blink as you placed it into your haversack, did the whiskers momentarily twitch? No, it was surely just your imagination. Even so, you waste no time in making your departure from this sinister cave.

*Add 1 to the score on your TREASURE COUNTER. Now hurry well away from this region by going to 136.*

### 235
### THIS CREATURE
### IS SLAIN BY

⟨**9**⟩

### WOUNDS

*Wage combat by simultaneously throwing the two dice. If you slay the creature, go to 197. If the creature inflicts a wound on you first, deduct 1 from your STRENGTH RATING and then flee well away from this region by hurrying to 136.*

### 236

You rap on the left-hand door a couple of times and then wait for an answer. There's a long delay but eventually you hear a slow shuffling behind the door and then the sound of the bolt being withdrawn. A furtive old man appears, barely visible underneath his hooded cloak. 'You need not explain what you want from me,' he croaks as he invites you into the shadows of his cave, misty with bubbling concoctions. 'Lay your shield on my experiment bench here and I will convert it back to iron. But you must turn your eyes away. No man must see how it is done.' So you do as he asks, turning your back on the experiment bench. A few minutes later the alchemist taps you on the shoulder, presenting you with your shield. Miraculously, it is of sturdy iron again!

*Add 1 to your STRENGTH RATING. Go next to 74.*

## 237
## THIS CREATURE IS SLAIN BY

⟨7⟩

## WOUNDS

*Wage combat by simultaneously throwing the two dice. If you slay the creature, go to 308. If the creature inflicts a wound on you first, deduct 1 from your STRENGTH RATING and then flee well away from this region by hurrying to 26.*

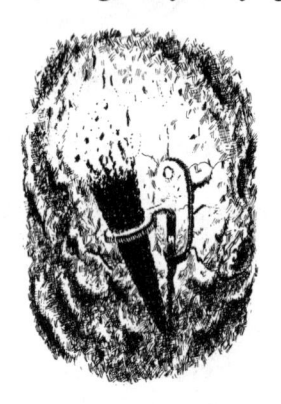

### 238

Just as you feel that you are about to collapse into the snaking streams of lava, you sense a waft of fresh air from ahead. Just in time, it seems that you have reached a much cooler pocket of the caves. But entering that delicious breeze isn't as easy as you had hoped, for two maidens in long white togas suddenly bar your path. 'One can only enter the cooling cave by speaking the correct password,' they tell you. 'It is one of three: *Tagel, Ruthlor* or *Kravix*. Which is it you choose?'

*If you have picked up the PASSWORD SCROLL on your*

*adventure, use it here to find out the correct password. If you don't have the SCROLL, you'll have to guess the correct password.*

> If you think it's TAGEL **go to 210**
> If you think it's RUTHLOR **go to 286**
> If you think it's KRAVIX **go to 252**

### 239

The dying creature desperately tries to produce one last jet of fire, snorting for all its worth. But it can only emit a weak puff of black smoke. It then seems to choke on this smoke, spluttering to the ground. When you are sure at last that it can do no further harm, you heave at the tomb's heavy stone lid again. The golden dagger, you are relieved to see, is just clear of the tomb's occupant. It's a few centimetres from the skeleton's right foot. So you carefully put in your hand to fish it out.

*Add 1 to the score on your TREASURE COUNTER. Now hurry well away from this region by going to 136.*

### 240

You soon realise that it was a mistake to try and wade through the whirlpool to the far side. The swirling water is already up to your chest level – and you're still less than a third of the way across. You desperately try to keep your footing on the slippery rocks beneath, but it's quite hopeless. The strong undercurrent suddenly seems to wrap around your ankles and drag them backwards. You're now being carried along in the turbulent water, your fate totally in its hands. It tosses you towards a series of sharp rocks jutting out along the side of the chasm . . . *Go to 225.*

### 241

The password you gave seems to be correct because the wizard lets you step into his small cave, feeling his way after you. He touches your arm and points to a series of dingy-looking jars on a stone shelf.

'The third from the right, please, Tronk,' he instructs you. As you fetch down this jar, however, brushing the cobwebs from its grimy stopper, you wonder whether you are wise to let this strange little man try and help you. This jar is by far the foulest looking of them all, containing a mould-encrusted jelly. 'Now don't grimace, Tronk,' the old man sniggers, sensing your reaction. 'They might not look very appealing but you know how miraculous my medicines always are!' So you decide to trust him, taking the large spoonful of the jelly he offers you. 'That serves your deception right!' he cries out, suddenly breaking into a loud cackle when he's heard you swallow it. 'Your password was wrong, stranger! This potion is boiled bat entrails and will weaken you even more!'

*Deduct 1 from your STRENGTH RATING. Go next to 145.*

### 242

They are the maidens' hands but they have suddenly become twice as large and strong, as a warrior's. Realising that you must have given the wrong password, you desperately fight for air as the two maidens try to submerge you. It's a fight you almost lose but you at last manage to prise their hands free, and yank them into the water. Coughing and spluttering for dear life, you crawl exhausted towards the cavern's exit.

*Deduct 1 from your STRENGTH RATING. Go next to 145.*

### 243

'So you feel you have a better chance with the beasts!' the dwarf remarks with a slight smirk on his face. It's as if he knows something that you don't. 'Well, we shall see,' he adds, hobbling up to the small rostrum in the centre of the sanded arena, 'we shall see. Let the parade of beasts begin!' He picks up a long leather whip from the rostrum and cracks it in the air. There's soon a creaking sound from the far side of the large arena and you notice that a tunnel emerges there, its entrance protected by a heavy portcullis. This portcullis is now slowly lifting and you can see a three-headed

reptile, saliva dripping from its trio of mouths. You guess that you must slice through all *three* heads if you are going to kill it. Cutting off only one – or even two – is unlikely to be sufficient.

| If you wish to fight creature | **go to 165** |
| If you wish to avoid it | **go to 12** |

### 244

As fast as you now dart across the stones, the explosion of fire is always just ahead of you, singeing your hair and skin every time you leap through the flaming wall. You try belatedly to do as the goblin advised and take a path away from the stones but you are strangely confined there, still having to leap from one fiery platform to the next. Although the other side of the swamp is now in sight, the heat has become unbearable and you're not sure you'll make it.

***Deduct 1 from your STRENGTH RATING. Go next to 106.***

### 245

You're wondering whether to defy the voice and climb down into the other pit to rescue your *rightful* shield when a gnome appears at your side. He seems to be able to read your mind because he sternly shakes his head at you. 'That other pit is now bottomless,' he warns you. 'If you were to climb into it, you would never be seen again. Don't despair, though. Come with me and I'll take you to the cave of the alchemist. If he can turn base metal into gold, which he does all the time, I'm sure he'll have no difficulty turning wood into base metal!' So, fairly confident that you can trust this gnome, you follow him towards the alchemist's cave. ***Go to 131.***

### 246

The water tastes delicious, cool and fresh. So you throw back your head even further, letting the drops fall right to the back of your throat. You wonder where this fresh water could have come from, deciding there must be a stream flowing along the top of the cliffs. Instead of dropping over the cliff edge as a small waterfall, it must have bored a hole somewhere along the cliff-top and seeped down this way. But you find it harder and harder to concentrate on the notion, your brain suddenly becoming very muzzy. The next thing you know you have dropped dizzily to the ground. Although you are able to stand up again several minutes later, you sense that your muscles have lost some of their strength. The water couldn't have been fresh after all. It must have been drugged.

***Deduct 1 from your STRENGTH RATING. Go next to 194.***

### 247

You now enter the last of the caves on the top row. Again, you cautiously raise the tomb's lid a fraction to find out what demon guards it. A glowing skull suddenly appears a few metres away from you, the glow becoming stronger and stronger. At first it has no eyes in its cavernous sockets but then a couple of piercing red orbs appear there. Then two claw-like hands, the left one bearing a hefty sword. Finally an armour-plated body grows beneath it, and a winged helmet frames its skull. The nightmarish creature beckons you, impatiently waiting for you to make your decision.

If you wish to fight creature **go to 73**
If you wish to avoid it **go to 136**

### 248

When you have climbed the thirty or so steps to the top row of caves, you warily start to investigate them. You enter the first cave, slowly approaching the huge stone tomb inside. Eerie shadows flicker across it from the candle burning hesitantly in the corner. Bracing yourself, you slowly raise the heavy lid of the tomb. There's a half-decayed skeleton inside, clad in leather armour, and you wonder if this is one of Sageor's brave but unsuccessful sons. This speculation is suddenly interrupted, though, when you spot an exquisite golden chalice at the feet of the skeleton. ***Go to 133.***

## 249

You have followed the central branch of the tunnel round several shadowy bends when you encounter a cramped cave hollowed out of the tunnel wall. Inside there's a long-bearded man dressed in a robe, sitting at a table, his bent back towards you. Regarding the items on this table – a skull, a large leather book, alchemy equipment – you guess him to be a wizard.

If you wish to enter cave **go to 342**
If you wish to continue past it **go to 145**

## 250

'So you think it's me who's lying, do you?' the hag on the right screams at you furiously. She yanks the ladle out of the cauldron and you duck, thinking that she is about to throw its steaming contents all over you. But she merely passes the ladle to the other hag, politely inviting her to do the stirring. She then turns to you, grinning, revealing horrible, decaying teeth. 'Well, you were right,' she admits simply, all the anger gone. 'It *was* me who was lying. I am the older by three hundred years. Our brew is nearly ready now so take some with you as a reward for settling our dispute.' Seeing all the frogs and small rodents swirling round in the cauldron, you decide to decline her offer. As hungry as you are, you would rather starve than take a mouthful of that foul concoction. ***Go to 101.***

## 251
## THIS CREATURE
## IS SLAIN BY

⟨5⟩

## WOUNDS

*Wage combat by simultaneously throwing the two dice. If you slay the creature, go to 113. If the creature inflicts a wound on you first, deduct 1 from your STRENGTH RATING and then flee well away from this region by hurrying to 136.*

## 252
The maidens coyly beckon you into the large cavern – so you assume your guess at the password must have been correct. They lead you past delicate sparkling waterfalls and ice-blue rock-pools. Long, slender reeds bend and sway in the cool breezes. It's the most tranquil and beautiful place you have ever beheld. 'Refresh yourself here,' one of the maidens speaks when they have led you to the edge of the largest of the rock-pools. But as you relax in the crystal clear water, closing your eyes, you suddenly feel two pairs of hands pressing down on your head . . . ***Go to 242.***

## 253
As the monster breathes its last, a final croak leaving its throat, you wipe your sword clean on some moss growing at the side of the tunnel. You then search for the diamond which fell from the monster's hand when you delivered that fatal wound. Ah, there it is – glinting near the creature's now still foot! After holding it up to the flickering light to admire its beauty, you put it into your haversack.

***Add 1 to the score on your TREASURE COUNTER. Now hurry well away from this region by going to 45.***

## 254

'You can see for yourself that this is not Cragcliff's crest on my shield,' you desperately try to persuade the urchin. 'I lied about being one of his bodyguards. I am here to destroy his kingdom.' At first the urchin examines your shield with the utmost suspicion but then his rage gradually calms. 'You speak the truth,' he admits. 'This is not Cragcliff's crest. That being so, I can perhaps be of some assistance to you.' ***Go to 42.***

## 255

Passing along the narrow walkway to the next cave, you again notice the sudden flickering of the candle as you enter. Your breathing must still be tense, heavy. Reassuring yourself that the creature lying in this tomb surely can't be quite as repulsive as the one you've just glimpsed, you slowly raise the heavy stone lid. But it *is* just as repulsive, perhaps even more so. Although its body is more or less human, its head is rat-like with crafty eyes and small razor-sharp teeth. These horrible teeth are suddenly revealed in full and the whiskers twitch as the creature slowly stirs to life. You quickly let the lid drop again to halt that process while you decide whether you wish to challenge it or not. For although transfixed by that abomination, you also couldn't help but notice the large, perfectly-cut diamond lying beside it.

> If you wish to fight creature  **go to 63**
> If you wish to avoid it  **go to 295**

### 256

At last you approach some light in the pyramid and you realise that you are at its centre. The illumination is provided by a narrow shaft of golden light which shines down through the dust from the pyramid's apex far above. It falls on a mummy's cast-iron tomb, which lies on a plinth just ahead of you. The illumination is exact, everything just beyond the tomb in total darkness. It's as if a fluorescent screen has been drawn closely round it. You've taken a couple of steps nearer to this tomb when a puff of green smoke suddenly appears to your left and hangs in mid-air. Then there's another puff to your right, this one red. ***Go to 105.***

### 257

The urchin shakes his head in sympathy as you discover that the chest is completely empty. 'If only I'd been able to help you!' he moans. He suddenly notices you move towards the other two chests. 'Don't open either of those!' he squeals in alarm. 'You can only have one attempt at choosing the right chest or you will bring disaster on my cave.' But his warning comes too late because you've already raised the lid of one of the other chests. Suddenly a large rock rolls towards the hole you entered by, completely sealing it. The great irony is that the tide of water has now completely passed through underneath, leaving the tunnel almost completely dry again. If it hadn't been for that huge rock, you could have immediately dropped down through the hole and continued on your journey. ***Go to 116.***

### 258

As the minotaur falls from the eighth stab of your sword, you wonder whether it will come to its final rest as a bull or man. Will it expire on its side or back? It breathes its last as a man, though, on its back. This is as you had hoped because such a position, flat nose facing upwards, makes it easier for you to tear out the gold ring. You drop it into your haversack and then leave the stone cage, slipping between the stalactite pillars again.

***Add 1 to the score on your TREASURE COUNTER. Now hurry well away from this region by going to 324.***

### 259
### THIS CREATURE
### IS SLAIN BY

⟨ **9** ⟩

### WOUNDS

***Wage combat by simultaneously throwing the two dice. If you slay the creature, go to 154. If the creature inflicts a wound on you first, deduct 1 from your STRENGTH RATING and then flee well away from this region by hurrying to 136.***

### 260

Leaving your sword and shield at the edge of the well on the left, you plunge into its warm water. Just for a moment you wonder whether it will in fact be warm, whether this is just a treacherous lure. But, however miraculous it seems, the water is like a shallow pool that has had the sun on it all day. Feeling the blood return to your veins, you could happily bask in there for hours. Ten minutes is all that you allow yourself, though. You sense that you are nearing the end of your quest and you are keen to reach that end as soon as possible. *Go to 334.*

### 261

The cloaked skeleton crumples to the ground. But you want to be absolutely sure that it is dead before attempting to remove the diamond pendant. So you press your foot to its chest while you push back its hood with your sword. The eyes are glinting no more. The creature is at rest. Its evil skull-face still unsettles you, however, and so you waste no time in tearing off the pendant and dropping it into your haversack.

*Add 1 to the score on your TREASURE COUNTER. Now hurry well away from this region by going to 136.*

### 262

You rap on the door in the centre a couple of times, waiting for an answer. When there isn't one, you try again – even louder this time. But again there's no answer and so you assume you must have picked the wrong door. This is confirmed when you turn the door's handle. To your surprise, it isn't locked – but to your disappointment you find that there's just an empty cave behind it. You notice that the goblin has now disappeared and you wonder whether you should try opening the other two doors. Even by force, if necessary. But you decide such an action would be foolish; you daren't risk angering the alchemist. If he can turn *wood* into base metal, then he might be able to do the same with flesh and bone! ***Go to 74.***

### 263

'Are you coward or crafty?' the dwarf shouts at you from the centre of the arena as another crack of his whip orders the hyena's departure. 'Is it that you are terrified by my first two beasts or do you think that by waiting you'll have an easier adversary?' He lets out a short, wheezy cackle, tossing back his head, and then abruptly cracks his whip again. The thin layer of sawdust on the arena scatters as a huge lizard emerges from the shadows of the tunnel, its heavy footsteps shaking the ground. Its head is like a dinosaur's, with a fearsome array of large pointed teeth, but these are not its only weapons. It possesses thick, razor-sharp claws and a massive leathery tail. Just the slightest swish of this would surely crush you to death.

If you wish to fight creature    **go to 299**
If you wish to avoid it    **go to 26**

## 264

You come out of the ice door in the centre feeling no stronger than you were before. You must have chosen the wrong one. Just before the door swings itself shut again, you jam your foot into the gap. The obvious thing to do, you think, would be to re-enter the temple and come out by one of the other doors. Perhaps the prophetesses wouldn't notice you. They did after all have their backs turned to the three doors. But then there returns to you that haunting image of what was underneath their hoods; the hideous skulls of ice. You decide that to try and cheat creatures like that would be most unwise. *Go to 74.*

## 265

'This river leads right out of the caves,' the wizard explains to you. 'Indeed, it's the only way out. But to take this boat you must give me the correct password. I can tell that you have come a long way through the caves, with many perilous adventures, and so I will give you a chance. The correct word is either *Cherlin*, *Torzad* or *Dradvil*.'

*If you have picked up the PASSWORD SCROLL during your adventure, you may consult it here to find out the correct password. If not, you'll have to hope for the best in making your choice.*

| | |
|---|---|
| If you think it's CHERLIN | **go to 76** |
| If you think it's TORZAD | **go to 202** |
| If you think it's DRADVIL | **go to 158** |

## 266

'Before you go,' the wretch's feeble voice gasps at you, 'down that goblet of blue liquid on the bench over there. The torturers use a drop every so often to revive their victims. If you drink the whole goblet, it will restore all the strength you have lost while dangling here. Quickly – drink!' You are about to follow your fellow prisoner's instruction, raising the goblet to your lips, but then you begin to wonder if this is a trap. Perhaps the blue liquid only weakens the body further. Perhaps the prisoner is trying to make you drink it just to ingratiate himself to his captors in the hope that they will set him free. Dare you trust him or not?

*If you have been taught the TRANCE SPELL during your adventure, you may cast it here to hypnotise the prisoner into telling you whether he is speaking the truth or not. To do this, place the TRANCE SPELL CARD exactly over the prisoner's 'mind square' below. If you haven't learnt the TRANCE SPELL, you'll have to hope for the best in deciding what to do.*

```
  I  M  L  N N L     R  S
  S  N  P  Q E M A      K
P G     L  G J     G    R
  T  H H I    E    E    U
U V  T  U O T         P  S
O     T  O R P E S      T
  E  E        M N U   V V
F F     L L N O    N    E
```

If you decide to trust prisoner        **go to 214**
If you decide not to trust him         **go to 338**


### 267

Clawing your way up on to a small ledge on the slippery rocks at the side of the whirlpool, you watch anxiously as the black, swirling water continues to rise. Will it never stop? Another half metre and it will start to submerge even your refuge. You desperately look for an even higher ledge but this is the best there is. Still the water rises and you are convinced that it will eventually cover your head. So you decide you're going to have to challenge it now while there's still a small chance of survival. It's the only way out. You suddenly plunge into the angry swirl, swimming frantically against it back towards the chasm's entrance. ***Go to 21.***

### 268

At first, you can't be sure whether you have struck the swamp-corpse fatally or not because it has no throat to howl and no eyes to roll. But its hideous grin slowly disappears and the twitching bones of its fingers start to fumble with the ruby in its sword, eventually prising it out. In dignified admission of its defeat, it tosses you the fiery jewel. Then the wretched creature seems to dissolve before your eyes, even its bones now without covering. Then there's just marrow from the middle of its bones, the yellowish jelly slowly dripping away into the swamp.

***Add 1 to the score on your TREASURE COUNTER. Now hurry well away from this region by going to 54.***

### 269

First there is a loud cackle of relieved laughter. Then the creaking winch yanks your feet even further from the ground. The two sounds tell you that your choice of password must have been wrong. Your captors now leave you to dangle there, their cruel laughter gradually fading away into distant echoes. The strain on your taut arms is immense, the pain soon becoming unbearable. It's not long before you pass out.

***Deduct 1 from your STRENGTH RATING. Go next to 146.***

## 270

Your reflection speaks the password as you do and you observe your anxiety in it as you wonder whether you have spoken correctly. Suddenly the pool loses its stillness, starting to ripple. The ripple soon becomes a fierce bubbling. Realising that you must have spoken the wrong password, you try to move away but you find yourself rooted to the spot. Then the bubbling water leaps out at you, pulling you in. You desperately try to keep your head above the raging swirl as it attempts to drown you. Just as you think you have lost the battle, the pool's fury subsides. It returns to its complete stillness once more. You have swallowed so much water, however, that you can barely drag yourself out.

***Deduct 1 from your STRENGTH RATING. Go next to 155.***

## 271

The fiend that materialises in the corner of the next cave is also armed with fire. Its weapon is a curved blade of flame. It brandishes it at you as you raise the lid of the tomb in there. The face behind the fiery sword is one of piercing deep set eyes and animal-like fangs. Its nostrils are widely and aggressively flared, moist with odious secretions. You could, of course, immediately make the abomination disappear by dropping the tomb's lid. Lying at the bottom of the tomb, though, is a small leather pouch. It's your guess that it contains either gold coins or jewels . . .

> If you wish to fight creature   **go to 28**
> If you wish to avoid it   **go to 247**

### 272
Your guess must have been correct because the portcullis suddenly starts to lift. It rises more slowly than it fell, however. At last it's just high enough for you to pass underneath and you unsuspectingly duck your head, walking through. But it's a trap – for the heavy gate suddenly comes crashing down on top of you. Crushed against the rocky ground, you try to utter one of the other passwords but you can't even breathe, let alone speak. Only after you have passed out does the portcullis start to lift again. Does it assume that you are dead? Perhaps you are . . .

***Deduct 1 from your STRENGTH RATING. Go next to 66.***

### 273
'Watch!' the Chief Sorcerer commands. 'You shall now glimpse the face of your enemy.' His features slowly dissolve, and the blue mist gradually changes to black. You watch with some trepidation, assuming that you will see Cragcliff's evil features. But just as the black mist looks as if it is about to take on another form, it suddenly explodes in your face. The tiny cave reverberates with evil, mocking laughter and you realise that you must have chosen the wrong password. You drop dizzily to your knees . . .

***Deduct 1 from your STRENGTH RATING. Go next to 15.***

### 274
You haven't followed the left branch of the tunnel very far when you suddenly hear a heart-stopping noise some distance behind

you. It's the sound of invading water – huge, thundering waves of it. Sure that it will completely flood the tunnel, you frantically look for an escape. As fortune has it, you suddenly spot two ropes dangling a short distance in front of you. They are about three metres apart, each leading up to a small arch-shaped hole in the tunnel roof. If you were to climb quickly up into one of the holes, you would surely be safe from the imminent torrent of water. ***Go to 167.***

### 275

'Ah, so Ugger doesn't appeal to you,' the dwarf shouts out. He cracks his whip again and the Neanderthal lumbers, snarling, back into the tunnel. 'You see, I have their total obedience,' the dwarf boasts proudly. 'I am their absolute master.' He cracks the whip again and a horned fiend now emerges from the tunnel's shadows,

as if it had come up from Hell itself. It hisses fire and evil black vapours from its nostrils, rending the air with its claws.

| | |
|---|---|
| If you wish to fight creature | **go to 237** |
| If you wish to avoid it | **go to 184** |

## 276

Walking to the left side of the massive cavern, you can't resist peering into some of the shadowy recesses which honeycomb its walls. The first is empty, the second merely contains a pool of stagnant water, but the third is like a hermit's cave. Instead of a hermit dwelling there, though, there are two wart-nosed hags. They are sitting on either side of a bubbling cauldron, squabbling over who should stir the evil-looking contents. Their black-toothed glee as they bicker suggests this is quite a common occurrence. *Go to 34.*

## 277

It takes a while for all claws to stop twitching but at last the giant crab is dead. Each claw is now clamped firmly together, never to do harm again. You still don't completely trust the huge pincers at the front, though, and so you climb on the creature's rock-like back to prise out the sapphire. It's the colour of the bluest sea and that is presumably where it originally came from. You can imagine Sageor's satisfied smile as you place the magnificent jewel into your haversack.

*Add 1 to the score on your **TREASURE COUNTER**. Now hurry well away from this region by going to 50.*

## 278

You hear the creature bellow after you as you forge deeper and deeper into the caves. But as its wail recedes another, coming from in front of you, grows louder. You start to tread more warily, squinting hard into the flickering shadows ahead for a glimpse of this second fiend. Your expectations rise every time you turn a bend but at each one you are disappointed. Surely it must be very close now, though, because the wail has become almost deafening in its intensity. But then it starts slowly to diminish. Bewildered, you retrace some of your steps, failing to understand how you could have passed the source of those cries. Ah, that's how! ***Go to 36.***

### 279

Waiting until the water has completely drained away, you cautiously re-enter the chasm. You hope that the whirlpool was just an occasional natural occurrence and not a recurring trap for anyone who ventures inside. Fortunately, this would seem to be the case, for although you are half-expecting it to repeat at every stride, that terrifying swell of water doesn't start up again. ***Go to 194.***

### 280

Stepping through the door on the right, you feel a freezing shiver run through your body. You've never known cold as extreme as this, it seeming many times more severe than even the rest of the ice cavern. But when it has passed, your body feels strangely refreshed, invigorated. It's as if you had never drunk from that lethal chalice.

***Add 1 to your STRENGTH RATING. Go next to 74.***

## 281

The mermaid shakes her head sadly at you as you completely ignore her warning. You shake your head back at her, though, sure that this is still part of her treachery. But your boat hasn't travelled very far along the left side of the river when it's suddenly dashed against the rocky walls of the tunnel. You're thrown out by the jolt, the fierce current swirling you round and round. You desperately try to swim against it but then it dashes *you* against the jagged wall as well, knocking you unconscious. When you finally come round, it's to find yourself floating in completely calm water again, much further down the river. Your boat is also floating there; upside-down but – miraculously – undamaged. As you clamber back into it, though, you suddenly feel as if you're about to pass out again. That blow to your head must have been very severe.

***Deduct 1 from your STRENGTH RATING. Go next to 39.***

## 282

To your disappointment, you find that the chest is empty. But need this be the cause of disappointment? Surely you can just move on to one of the other two chests. The face in the water has now disappeared – and so you can't see that there's anything to stop you. To save time, you give each chest a quick shake. The first is silent but the second rattles as if there's something rolling about inside. When you open the lid, however, you're bewildered to discover that this one is also completely empty. It's obviously not as easy as you had thought to cheat the mysterious face! ***Go to 312.***

## 283
## THIS CREATURE IS SLAIN BY

⟨8⟩

### WOUNDS

*Wage combat by simultaneously throwing the two dice. If you slay the creature, go to 86. If the creature inflicts a wound on you first, deduct 1 from your STRENGTH RATING and then flee well away from this region by hurrying to 136.*

### 284

As you pass to the right of the ice temple, you come across three wells. Their walls are constructed of small blocks of ice, laid like bricks, but strangely the water within this circle of ice hasn't frozen. Indeed, the water seems to be heated because steam is rising from each well. Your shivering body tantalised by this, you decide to take a dip in one of the wells. But which should you choose? They all seem to be identical – even having the same design chiselled round their rims, depicting birds and nymphs.

*If you have picked up the BOOK OF WISDOM during your adventure, you may consult it here to find out which well to choose. If not, you'll have to hope for the best in making your decision.*

| | |
|---|---|
| If you choose well on left | **go to 200** |
| If you choose well in centre | **go to 144** |
| If you choose well on right | **go to 260** |

## 285

You wonder whether your decision to explore the beach is just an excuse; to delay your entry into that terrifying chasm for a while. Perhaps you should be honest with yourself – all those bloodcurdling howls have dented your courage a little. But you convince yourself that you made this decision to investigate the beach for a good reason. Maybe you'll find something amongst the shingle that will be of assistance to you in your adventure. Perhaps something dropped by one of the previous warriors who came here . . . ***Go to 57.***

## 286

'I'm afraid *Ruthlor* is wrong,' one of the maidens tells you shyly, staring at her feet. 'You cannot enter the cooling cave.' But you don't honestly see what these coy maidens can do to stop you and so, as courteously as you can, you pass between them into the large cavern. It's the most tranquil place you have ever seen. Trickling down from light shafts far above, fine waterfalls sparkle ice-green across exotic leaves and tendrils growing on the rocks. But suddenly the waterfalls change to a muddy brown and when you turn to look at the maidens again, you see that their frail faces are no more. There's now a hideous hag under each shawl. In horror, you run for the far exit from the cave but you reach it only after the hags have mumbled a chant after you. You immediately begin to feel a strange sapping of your strength.

***Deduct 1 from your STRENGTH RATING. Go next to 145.***

## 287

You squeeze along the narrow walkway to the next cave. Again, there's a large stone tomb in its centre and, again, you wonder if it contains one of Sageor's brave sons. You're a bit more hesitant about easing up the lid this time, though, in case exactly the same thing occurs as last time. It does . . . and a horned fiend suddenly appears in the corner. The horns seem to be everywhere; sprouting not just from either side of its head but also from its shoulder blades, elbows and knees. You wonder if these horns are its only weapon. If they are, then it might be quite an easy opponent. But then suddenly it blows a jet of fire from each nostril. You quickly glance inside the tomb before deciding whether to let the lid down and make the creature disappear. You spot a solid gold dagger lying at the bottom . . .

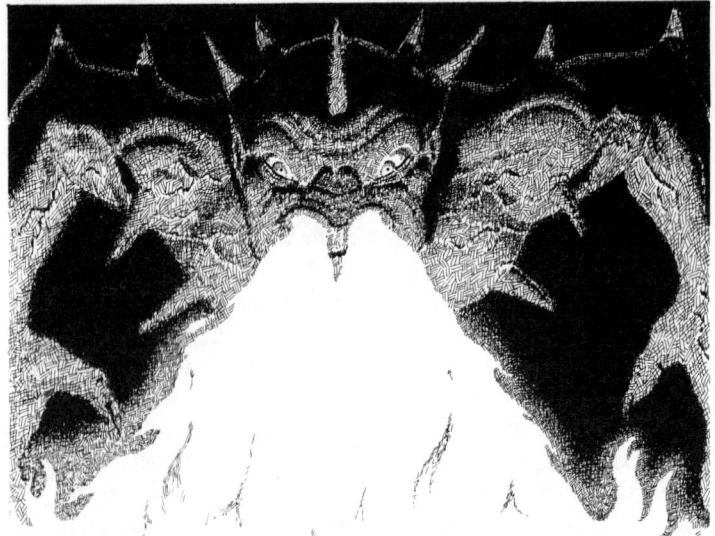

> If you wish to fight creature     **go to 95**
> If you wish to avoid it     **go to 271**

## 288

As long as you're careful to avoid each eleventh stepping-stone, you assume you should have no problem getting right across the swamp. The goblin has thankfully disappeared, unwilling or unable to try and cause you any further mischief. But as you count out the hundredth stepping-stone, you suddenly notice a stone bridge ahead. This bridge takes the place of the stepping-stones for a short distance but you somehow sense that the passage across it won't be straightforward. *Go to 77.*

### 289

'Ah, just as I suspected, dog!' the goblin sneers with joy and relief. 'You were lying!' He chuckles unpleasantly as he squats down on the raft, watching your head disappear under the swamp. But with one last massive effort, you swim under the slime towards his raft, surfacing on its far side. You stealthily pull yourself on to it, creeping up behind the goblin as he delightedly prods his punt-pole at the spot where you disappeared. You suddenly charge into his back and knock the nasty little wretch into the swamp. But you're unable to gloat at his demise, for that arduous underwater swim took every last bit of strength out of you and you collapse on to the raft.

*Deduct 1 from your STRENGTH RATING. Go next to 49.*

### 290

Even if you *have* chosen the wrong arch, you are convinced that you can pass through it quickly enough to avoid whatever dangers it might hide. But as you step into the arch, you realise that it's much deeper than it appeared. The other end is a good fifteen metres away. You immediately make a dash for this other end but you're less than halfway there when the rocky walls on either side of you suddenly start to exude a thick, bluish vapour. You clap a hand to your nose and mouth, trying to avoid inhaling the vapour, but it quickly invades your lungs. You desperately stagger onwards, knowing that if you don't get out of this noxious arch you will almost certainly perish.

*Deduct 1 from your STRENGTH RATING. Go next to 58.*

## 291
## THIS CREATURE IS SLAIN BY

⟨**9**⟩

## WOUNDS

*Wage combat by simultaneously throwing the two dice. If you slay the creature, go to 31. If the creature inflicts a wound on you first, deduct 1 from your STRENGTH RATING and then flee well away from this region by hurrying to 136.*

## 292
You've ventured only a few metres into the exit on the left when you find the pitcher of oil. You do as the mysterious voice instructed, smearing the oil over your arms, chest and legs. As you wait for it to have its effect you only hope the voice can be trusted. You start to worry that it might have deceived you and the oil will weaken you even more. But then a surge of strength seems to run through you, your muscles soon feeling completely invigorated.

*Add 1 to your STRENGTH RATING. Go next to 157.*

## 293
Your branch of the river now enters a much larger tunnel and it's here that you join the other two branches. The three branches now flow together, the current becoming a little faster. It soon becomes

much faster and you worry that your boat might be overturned. You're just wondering whether to follow a course to the left or right side of the river when a soft voice calls out to you. It's a mermaid sitting on a rock. 'Steer to the right-hand side,' she warns. 'If you don't, you will be drowned.' Knowing how treacherous mermaids can be, however, you wonder if you should trust her.

*If you have been taught the TRANCE SPELL during your adventure, you may cast it here to hypnotise the mermaid into telling you whether she spoke the truth. To do this, place the TRANCE SPELL CARD exactly over her 'mind square' below. If you haven't been taught the TRANCE SPELL, you'll have to hope for the best in making your decision.*

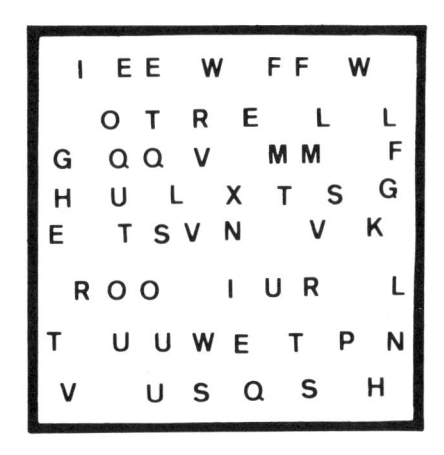

```
    I   E E   W     F F    W
        O  T  R   E     L       L
   G   Q Q   V     M M          F
   H   U   L   X   T   S        G
   E    T S V  N       V        K

        R O O      I   U R      L

   T    U U W E    T   P        N
   V       U S Q   S   H
```

If you decide to steer to the left    **go to 281**
If you decide to steer to the right    **go to 80**

## 294

You crawl into the shaft on the right but then stop for a moment, calling back to the urchin. You ask him if he's sure he won't join you. But he must be in a sulk because there's no reply. So you decide to let him get on with it and continue your crawl through the narrow tunnel. It remains perfectly horizontal for the first fifty metres or so but then it starts to slope downwards. A short while later you find yourself emerging into the main tunnel . . . back where you started, directly underneath the urchin's hole again. As you peer up at the large rock now blocking that hole, you rather guiltily picture that poor wretch sitting trapped behind it. You again regret that he didn't come with you along the shaft. ***Go to 330.***

## 295

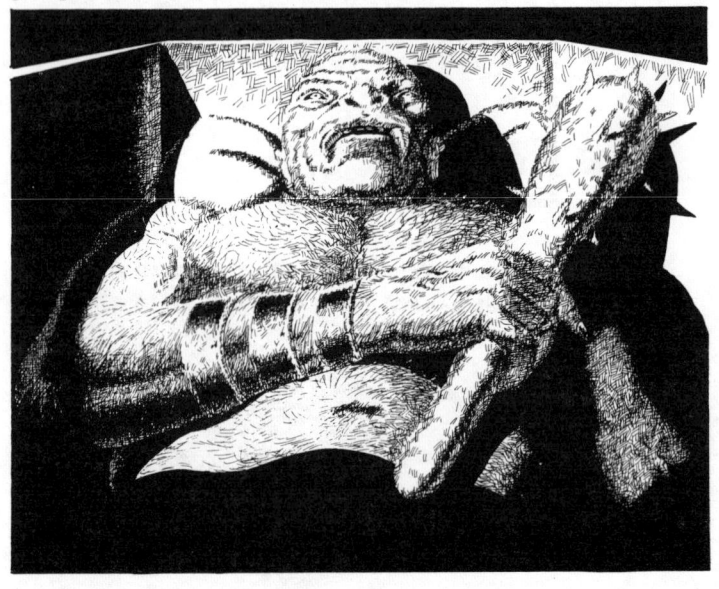

Wondering whether you will regret not challenging the rat creature for that diamond, you now enter the last cave along this middle row. Surely the creature in this tomb will be less ghastly to look at? In some ways it is – for when you warily lift the stone lid a fraction you glimpse a sort of caveman inside. True, its face is more that of an aggressive beast's than a man's – with hyena-like eyes and a massive fang at each corner of its mouth – but the sight is not quite as repulsive as that you have just witnessed. If the creature is slightly less of an abomination to look at, however, that's not to say it doesn't appear just as strong. Its arms are covered in hair, and bulging with muscle, and there's a vicious, spiked club in its oversized hand. Just above this hand, though, there are three armlets of solid gold . . .

> If you wish to fight creature      **go to 235**
> If you wish to avoid it      **go to 136**

### 296

You tensely put your foot on to the narrow crossing, ready to whip it back if there is the slightest sign of the bridge suddenly crumbling away. It seems very secure, though, and so you risk the whole of your weight on it. You're sure now that you have chosen the correct bridge. Didn't the mason say that the wrong one would collapse as soon as someone stepped on it? And you now hear that odd little creature cursing you behind your back, angrily brandishing his hammer and chisel. When you reach the very centre of the bridge, however, his cursing ominously changes to a gleeful chuckle. Alarmed, you try to dash for the other end of the bridge but the whole thing suddenly disintegrates. You fall headlong into the chasm.

***Deduct 1 from your STRENGTH RATING. Go next to 55.***

## 297

Concerned that you might have chosen the wrong one, you barely sip the liquid in the chalice. But the prophetess becomes angry, raising her head. To your horror, you see that there *isn't* a face there, just a skull of ice. The eye sockets glisten with her anger. 'If you don't drink,' she warns you, 'your fate will be much worse. This ice temple will turn to fire and you will be burnt to ashes. Us too – so do as I command. Now drink!' No sooner have you emptied the chalice than you collapse to the floor. You lie there helpless, conscious only of that beguiling chant above you. But then even that begins to fade . . .

***Deduct 1 from your STRENGTH RATING. Go next to 319.***

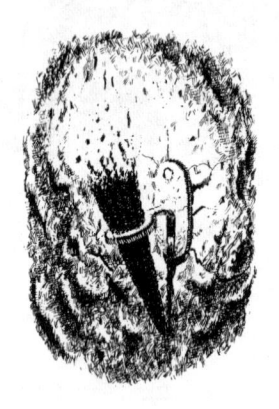

## 298

You haul yourself up into the hole just in time. The surge of water suddenly comes crashing through the tunnel, reaching to within only half a metre of your refuge. If you had been still standing on the floor of the tunnel, you would surely have drowned. Peering down from your hole, you wait for the fierce swell of water to pass through – and, rather strangely, this happens much sooner than you expect. It appears to be just a single tidal wave, with nothing behind it. Indeed, within minutes the tunnel is almost completely dry again. After waiting a little longer just to make absolutely sure there's no more to follow, you slither back down the rope. ***Go to 330.***

## 299
## THIS CREATURE IS SLAIN BY

⟨8⟩

## WOUNDS

*Wage combat by simultaneously throwing the two dice. If you slay the creature, go to 98. If the creature inflicts a wound on you first, deduct 1 from your STRENGTH RATING and then flee well away from this region by hurrying to 26.*

### 300

You expect to be immediately pounced on from either side but the chasm's shadows are still and quiet. Too quiet, all of a sudden . . . this is surely just to draw out your suspense, put your nerves even more on edge. There is one slight sound, though – the slow drip, drip of water from directly above you. You wonder if this might be fresh water. There's nothing you crave for more after all that seawater you have swallowed. But dare you risk throwing back your head to taste the drips? The water might be contaminated.

| If you wish to drink the water | **go to 246** |
| If you decide it better not to | **go to 124** |

### 301

Still not turning round to take a look at you, the old man slowly nods his silver head. 'Well done,' he says softly. 'Now for my first instruction,' he adds, leafing through the tattered pages of his book. 'Scrape off some of the lichen growing at the entrance to my cave and smear it on your tongue. It will give you a rare power. I wish you to go now, though. My old head is tired.' As you leave the wizard's cave, you smile to yourself at how you had deceived this secret out of him. But you soon find out that it was the cunning old wizard who had deceived *you*. For no sooner have you smeared the green mould on your tongue as he'd instructed, than you feel a weakening of your arms and legs. That password you gave him couldn't have been the right one after all!

***Deduct 1 from your STRENGTH RATING. Go next to 145.***

### 302

As you move towards the left well, you suddenly find that the invisible hand is gone. You wonder if you had just imagined it, whether it was your dizziness playing cruel tricks on you. You rather doubtfully begin to turn the rusty winch. The chain winds round and round, but still there's no sign of a bucket at its end. In fact, you're beginning to wonder if the chain has an end. Finally, though, you can hear a faint clattering from down the well as the bucket knocks against its sides, slowly making its way to the surface. As soon as you can reach it, you scoop out some of the stagnant water inside, trickling it over your head as you had been instructed. For a moment there's nothing . . . but then your dizziness suddenly clears.

***Add 1 to your STRENGTH RATING. Go next to 157.***

### 303

The heavy portcullis remains firmly on the ground and so you assume your guess at the password must have been wrong. You stand there anxious, desperate, wondering what to do next. Unless you can find some way of getting past it, your quest can go no further. It ends right here. There seems only one thing for it – you're going to have to try and lift the portcullis. So you drop into a squat, slipping your hands under the small gap at the bottom of the iron barrier . . . ***Go to 186.***

### 304

Moving on from the rocky cage, you arrive at two more; one to the left of you and one to the right. Here too there are enraged creatures, pounding their fists and skulls against the stalactite bars. You go to investigate the creature on the right first. A hybrid head – half gorilla, half human – sits atop a beast's hairy trunk. It lashes out razor-sharp claws at you as you approach a little too near to its stalactite prison. You leap back just in time. However, that brief proximity to its cage enabled you to catch a glimpse of a dazzling diamond in there and you wonder whether you should squeeze through the protective row of stalactites to challenge the creature for its treasure.

> If you wish to fight creature     **go to 176**
> If you wish to avoid it     **go to 75**

## 305

As you open the chest on the left, a yellowish vapour curls out. Immediately realising that you must have chosen the wrong one, you slam the lid shut again. But even a whiff of that noxious smoke seems to have been enough for it to produce its devastating effect. Your legs suddenly go weak, you start to sway. If you grow any dizzier then you probably won't even be able to make it to the other side of the bridge. You'll just topple over into the ravine . . .

***Deduct 1 from your STRENGTH RATING. Go next to 20.***

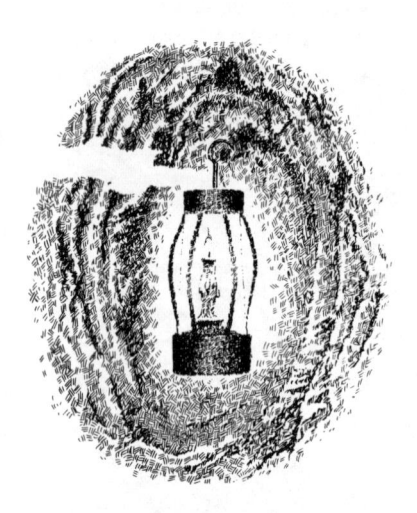

## 306

When you finally come round, it is to see a dirty goblin-like face peering down at you. The creature is much smaller than a goblin, though, and is dressed in filthy rags. You guess that it is some form of urchin. He prods you with a disdainful finger. 'Who are you?' he demands. 'What are you doing in my chimney cave? Answer! Or I'll set my bats on you again!' You begin by telling him the truth – that you had climbed up here to seek refuge from the sudden tidal wave. But then you decide it best to follow with a lie, claiming to be one of Cragcliff's bodyguards. Instead of your statement gaining respect from him, however, it sends the grubby little creature into a foul-mouthed rage. ***Go to 5.***

## 307

Steering your boat towards the arch on the left, you now paddle it inside. The tunnel echoes with the drips of water from your oars as you look out for any danger. Fortunately, the flaming torches continue into this tunnel, although they become less frequent than they were before. Suddenly, though, there's a bright glow ahead. At first you delightedly assume it to be daylight but then you realise that it's a strange ball of bluish mist approaching you. *Go to 99.*

## 308

The dwarf screams all sorts of curses at you as the monster falls from your last sword thrust. With an almighty thud it crashes on to the arena's light surface of sand. It doesn't even twitch. It's stone dead. 'How dare you! How dare you!' the dwarf screams wildly, stamping his foot. 'It was *you* who were meant to die.' Tearing the sapphire ring from his finger, he protects it in his little fist as he sees you approach him. He might have done better to have picked up his whip, though, for it's the easiest thing in the world to wrest your rightful prize from the bad sport.

*Add 1 to the score on your TREASURE COUNTER. Now hurry well away from this region by going to 26.*

**309**

As you follow round the right side of the cavern, you peer up at all the small caves in the rock. There are three levels of them, some with candles flickering inside but most dark. As your eye rises to the very top level, you suddenly spot a small hunched shadow beckoning you towards his dwelling. Curious, you scramble up the rock. 'Step inside, step inside!' the strange creature welcomes you when you finally reach his cave. He has a huge, warty nose poking out from a shabby green hood. You recognise in him the unmistakable filth and ugliness of a cave gnome. *Go to 135.*

**310**

'Well, you can't have had that bad a knock on the head, Tronk,' the old man giggles at you, 'if you can still remember the password!' Relieved that your guess was right, you follow the funny little creature into his small cave. But his giggle suddenly turns into an angry snarl. 'But of course you're *not* Tronk, are you?' he snaps. 'You're not my manservant. You're an imposter! Your password was wrong!' He quickly feels his way towards a bottle of liquid on his medicine table, dashing it into your face. 'That's what you get for deceiving me, stranger!' he says, cackling unpleasantly. 'Far from giving you something to restore your strength, I've doused you with a potion that will make it even weaker!'

*Deduct 1 from your STRENGTH RATING. Go next to 145.*

## 311

Entering by the arch on the left, you find yourself in total darkness. Then a gentle glow appears and you discover that it comes from two strange and luminous statues, one on either side of you. They both have the bodies of ancient Egyptians but the one on the left has the head of an ass and the one on the right the head of a bird of prey. Continuing past these mysterious monuments, walking through darkness once more, it occurs to you how illusory this pyramid is. From the outside it looked quite small. But on the inside it seems to have almost infinite depth. ***Go to 256.***

## 312

The river continues to babble and gurgle through the caves, conveying you gently onward. You're just thinking that you can leave it all to the boat from now on when you notice that the river splits up into three branches ahead, each branch disappearing into an arched tunnel. As you approach the arches, wondering which one you should steer towards, you see that there's a large carving above them. A beautiful design of nymphs and flowers has been chiselled into the rock.

***If you have picked up the BOOK OF WISDOM during your adventure, you may consult it here to find out which arch you should enter. If not, you'll have to hope for the best in making your decision.***

|  |  |
|---|---|
| If you choose left arch | **go to 307** |
| If you choose centre arch | **go to 340** |
| If you choose right arch | **go to 35** |

**313**

Your reflection momentarily ripples as you toss the pebble into the pool. Then the perfect image returns, speaking independently of you once again. 'You have chosen correctly,' it says, 'your strength will be restored to you.' But do you trust it? You certainly don't feel a sudden surge of strength. Then you notice your reflection slowly move away from you and you realise that it's because you have effortlessly risen to your feet again. Your reflection was telling the truth; your lost strength has suddenly come back to you.

*Add 1 to your **STRENGTH RATING**. Go next to 157.*

**314**

No sooner have you yelled out Cragcliff's name than the goblin vanishes. He's clearly terrified of the monsters. You silently and anxiously wait for them to appear, staring across the swamp's hanging mists. Five minutes pass, ten, but still there is no sign of them. The surface of the swamp starts bubbling, the bubbles growing more and more violent. A grotesque creature suddenly erupts from the mire, dripping with black tangles of weed and slime.

Although horror-stricken by the sight, you still have the presence of mind to note its one possible handicap. The fingers round its sword are webbed. So do you wade in to fight the creature – or do you wait for its partner to make its appearance?

> If you wish to fight creature     **go to 149**
> If you wish to avoid it     **go to 180**

### 315

Squawking hideously, its feathers flying everywhere, the monstrous bird recoils from your final sword thrust. Its wings flap desperately in the air, trying to support its crumpling weight, but they become weaker and weaker. At last, they give out completely and the demonic creature drops like a stone into the depths of the chasm. You now again reach down for the golden egg, grasping it with care in case it goes the same way as the bird. When you have safely lifted it up, you allow yourself a few seconds to marvel at your gleaming prize before putting it into your haversack.

*Add 1 to the score on your TREASURE COUNTER. Now hurry well away from this region by going to 50.*

### 316

You climb up into the hole in the roof just in time because only a minute or so later the unit of warriors passes underneath you. Your calculation was right – there are about twenty of them. Built like oxen, they carry an assortment of terrifying weapons: swords, studded clubs, maces. You are waiting for them to get well ahead of you when you suddenly hear buzzing from the shadows of your refuge. A moment later it has grown into a deafening hum. It's a swarm of giant bees. The whole cave seems to vibrate with the terrifying sound as they start to attack. You desperately try to ward them off but they swoop on you, stinging your arms, face and neck. Although you finally manage to escape them by sliding down the rope again, you find that you can barely move because of all the swelling and pain.

*Deduct 1 from your STRENGTH RATING. Go next to 33.*

### 317

There's a short silence after you have made your guess at the password and you wonder whether it was right or not. It appears that it was correct because you suddenly hear the winch start to creak again. They must be letting you down. But, no, they're not – they're raising you even higher! Your password must have been wrong. Laughing at your pathetic attempt to deceive them, the brutes now leave the dungeon. The strain on your shoulders and arms as you are left to dangle there is horrendous, and each excruciating second seems a whole hour. It's not long before you pass out . . .

*Deduct 1 from your STRENGTH RATING. Go next to 146.*

### 318

At last you spot a pin-prick of light ahead. It grows stronger and stronger and you realise that you are approaching another open chamber. 'Is that my next guest?' a strange, high-pitched voice greets you as you step out into this large cavern. There's a dwarf looking you up and down, his hands placed self-importantly on his hips. 'It's been quite a wait. This is the Arena of Monsters and

Beasts and I am master of the arena. This sapphire ring you see on my finger is the most dazzling you've ever beheld, is it not? If you defeat any of my creatures, then it is yours. But first you must choose monster or beast. Then I will parade them for you, one by one.'

> If you choose monster      **go to 114**
> If you choose beast      **go to 243**

### 319

You gradually become conscious of the chant again – it's at first very vague, dream-like, but then it becomes rather clearer. It's as if it is bringing you round. 'It is not our wish that you die,' you hear the prophetess speak once more. 'The potion in that chalice was merely to weaken you. Indeed, even that punishment may be reversed if you leave our sacred temple immediately. But you must leave by the right exit. There are three doors to choose from behind us but only one of them will restore your strength. Choose wisely.' Finding the three doors, you see that they, too, are made of ice and that carved into this ice is a glistening design of flowers and nymphs.

***If you have picked up the BOOK OF WISDOM during your adventure, you may consult it here to find out the correct door to leave by. If not, you'll have to hope for the best in making your decision.***

> If you choose door on left      **go to 29**
> If you choose door in centre      **go to 264**
> If you choose door on right      **go to 280**

## 320

The goblin shakes his gnarled little fist at you as you step on to the tenth stepping-stone. It's as stable as the previous nine. But will the eleventh be just as stable? Just in case, you leap straight across it, just reaching the twelfth. The goblin again shakes his fist at you from the edge of the swamp. You immediately realise why; the eleventh stepping-stone has suddenly submerged into the slime. If you had landed on it, as the goblin had intended, then you would almost certainly have drowned. You half smile as the disgruntled evil little creature turns his back on you and walks away from the swamp. *Go to 288.*

## 321

As you cautiously make your way towards the right side of the tomb, you wonder if the laughter from the puff of green smoke – the one whose advice you ignored – will fade or grow louder. If it fades, it will surely mean that you did right to ignore it. But if it grows louder, it will surely mean that you did wrong! But its cackle remains exactly at the same level as it was before – and so does that from the puff of red smoke. They simply won't give you a clue one way or the other. So you tensely hold your breath and brush right past the tomb. *Go to 183.*

## 322

You now come to the last cave on this bottom row. The effigy lying on the tomb is again of a warrior but this one is female. She is young and slim but what she lacked in strength she appeared to make up for in skill and speed. There is a belt of deadly daggers round her waist and another dagger at each of her ankles. But as skilful as she might have been with these daggers, she, too, obviously failed in her quest. You sadly touch her stone face – but it immediately loses its beauty and youth, changing to the crumpled, leathery features of an old hag. Vipers appear in her hair and a grotesque lizard-like tongue spews from her mouth. It grows and grows and you're not sure which is going to be more venomous and lethal; this lashing tongue or the snakes.

> If you wish to fight creature **go to 182**
> If you wish to avoid it **go to 136**

### 323

As the creature sinks to the ground, howling in agony from your final sword thrust, you wonder where your prize is to be found. It's certainly not on the creature itself – but nor does it seem to be anywhere nearby. Cragcliff must have lied to you when he promised you his diamond! Incensed that the fiend is not honourable to his word, you climb back into your boat. You angrily start paddling towards that shaft of daylight again. But as you hear the wounded creature finally expire behind you – a last despairing wail echoing through the caves – something suddenly drops down into your boat. Cragcliff is true to his promise after all. It's his diamond – and by far the most magnificent you've ever seen!

***Add 1 to the score on your TREASURE COUNTER. Now hurry well away from this region by rowing to 120.***

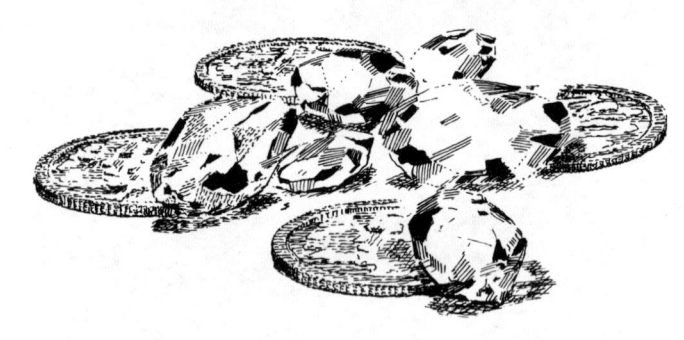

### 324

Your exploration of the echoing caverns continues, your hand clasped firmly to the hilt of your sword ready for your next encounter. But when it arrives the challenge is one where a sword can't assist you for it comes not in the form of aggressive beast or monster but a large swamp. Perhaps it has been created by water seeping up from underground or perhaps by moisture dripping down from above and gradually collecting over hundreds of years. But either way, a massive algae-covered lake stretches out in front of you, disappearing into swirling mists. The thick green slime of its surface lies eerily motionless, giving not the slightest indication of its depth. It might be just a few centimetres – or it might be treacherously deceptive and slurp and squelch without bottom. ***Go to 206.***

### 325

Emerging from the tunnel, you find yourself walking into the eeriest cavern of all. It's a cavern of catacombs; the high rocky wall on its left side gouged with a number of small caves. Each cave, dimly glowing from a single candle, contains a stone tomb. There are three rows of these shadowy caves, one on top of the other, access to them being via a series of steep steps. You are very much inclined to pass straight through this cavern but then you notice a huge inscription carved into the rock above the very top row of tombs. *Go to 97.*

### 326
'My first instruction to you,' the old man says, poring over the large leather-bound book in front of him, 'is how to use the trance spell. If you ever wonder whether a being is telling you the truth or not – or he is reluctant to tell you what you require – the trance spell will hypnotise him into helplessly surrendering that truth or information.' Floating his hands in the air, curling his fingers, the old man now proceeds to show you how to cast this spell. You watch intently, praying that he won't glance round until he has finished his demonstration. 'Can you remember all that?' he asks, at last turning to look at you. But it's too late – you are scurrying away from his cave, his valuable secret now yours as well.

*You may pick up the TRANCE SPELL card. Go next to 145.*

### 327
As you scramble up the steps they turn more and more to the left – away from the other set. You have climbed at least fifty steps now and you realise just how deep down in the island you are. There's not the slightest indication that you might soon surface into daylight. Even when the steps finally end, you feel just as much in the bowels of the island as you were before. You're now in another tunnel and you cautiously explore its twists and turns. Tapping your sword along the dark, rocky wall, you suddenly come across the arched entrance to a cave on your right. *Go to 18.*

### 328

The creature tries to tear the helmet from its skull as it reels from your final sword thrust. But then you realise that it is doing something much worse than this. It's trying to tear off its skull too – to bring about its end as quickly as possible. All you can do is watch in horror as the creature flings itself against the rocky walls of the cave. You turn away with revulsion as the skull finally comes free, rolling towards you. Not wishing to remain amidst this gory carnage a moment longer than necessary you quickly lift the lid of the tomb again to search out its treasure. You can't miss it. Sparkling brightly on one of the dead warrior's skeletal fingers is a huge diamond ring.

*Add 1 to the score on your TREASURE COUNTER. Now hurry well away from this region by going to 136.*

### 329

Warily stepping through the temple, you find yourself amongst wafting incenses and violet shadows. There's a blur of white ahead and, as you approach, you see that it is an altar attended by two prophetesses. Their white hooded gowns drape them from head to floor and you're not even sure there's anything more to them than these gowns. Both face and hands, if there be any, are lost in the white folds. It is from these folds that the chanting comes, drawing you irresistibly towards it. *Go to 233.*

### 330

As you resume your exploration of the tunnel, you are still in wonder at that strange tidal wave. It came and went, leaving nothing in its wake except a thin layer of damp sand on the tunnel floor. Or did it? For with consternation you notice that something has left a deep trail in the sand; something obviously very big and heavy. Turning a corner, you suddenly come across this creature. It's a giant crab! As its stalked eyes spot you, it snaps a huge claw in

your direction. The sight is quite terrifying. Anyone caught in that claw would surely be snapped like a twig. But there's quite an incentive for taking that awesome risk. The eye at the end of one of those stalks is not an eye at all but a sparkling sapphire.

If you wish to fight creature **go to 227**
If you wish to avoid it **go to 121**

### 331

As you withdraw your sword from the writhing octopus, there's a sudden discharge of black ink. This is its last desperate assault before its flailing tentacles drop limply to the ground. They then wither, curling tighter and tighter towards the creature's body. Some of the barnacles flake off as the tentacles shrink – and you watch carefully in case the emerald comes away as well. You're relieved to see that it does. You hadn't been relishing the prospect of sinking your sword into that leathery flesh again and possibly drawing yet another flood of ink.

*Add 1 to the score on your TREASURE COUNTER. Now hurry well away from this region by going to 50.*

### 332

Opening the chest in the middle, you are relieved to see that it is completely empty. No deadly scorpion crawls on to your hand and no poisonous vapour wafts out. But as you shut the lid again, you suddenly feel your legs start to wobble. Then you hear the mason's gloating cry behind you. 'So you are an enemy of these caverns!' he shouts. 'I hope for your sake that you are strong enough to withstand that transparent potion that was smeared on the lid. Otherwise,' he adds with a cruel laugh, 'you won't be able to help toppling off my bridge and plunging to your doom!'

*Deduct 1 from your STRENGTH RATING. Go next to 20.*

### 333

The creature sinks to the ground with an almighty moan. It writhes for a few moments, twitches slightly, and then is still. Then, miraculously, it changes back to stone. You are somewhat relieved at this, much preferring to prise the diamond from stone than fleshy eye-socket. So, using the hilt of your sword as a hammer, you chip away at the grotesque face and at last free the dazzling gem. You put it carefully into your haversack before continuing on your way.

*Add 1 to the score on your TREASURE COUNTER. Now hurry well away from this region by going to 109.*

## 334

Leaving the well behind you, you soon – mercifully – find yourself approaching a warmer draught of air. You must be about to leave the ice cavern. Exit from the cavern is, in fact, by one of two dark tunnels. They are only five metres apart and look almost identical but you wonder whether one might conceal a trap. You must choose wisely.

*If you have acquired INFRA-RED POWER during your adventure, you may employ it here to see through the darkness of the tunnels. To do this place the INFRA-RED POWER CARD exactly over the arched 'entrances' below. If you haven't acquired INFRA-RED POWER, you will have to hope for the best in making your choice.*

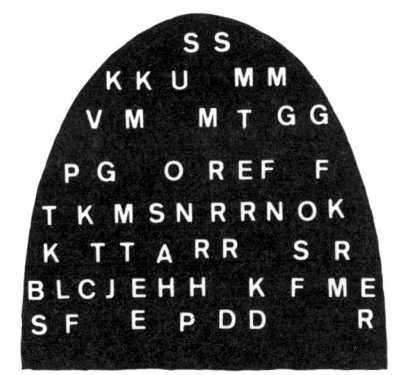

```
       S S                          F F  C E
   K K U   M M                  B D   A C D B
   V M   M T G G                E N   T     I N

  P G   O R E F   F             T P S O    R P     U
T K M S N R R N O K             D DN  H E E H  O R S
K  T T A R R     S R            R D E E  A H G    J J S
B L C J E H H  K F M E          H   H  A I A M M    K
S F    E  P D D        R        T B   J B F  G P E    T
```

|  |  |
|---|---|
| If you choose left tunnel | **go to 30** |
| If you choose right tunnel | **go to 110** |

### 335

Although the chasm on the right doesn't appear to be the easiest part to land at, the rocky shore looking particularly treacherous there, at least it's the nearest of the three. So you start to row towards this chasm, hoping you can steer a safe path through all the rocks. But there are even more rocks than you had thought, for many are hidden just below the water's surface. By the time you have realised, though, you are right amongst them and you hold your breath as there's one terrifying rasp after another on the bottom of your boat. Just as it's looking as if you have luckily survived all these, your craft is suddenly ripped at the stern. You quickly plunge into the water and turn your boat over so it won't sink, but guiding it all the way to the shore takes an incredible toll on your strength. With your arms and legs badly gashed by the rocks, you lay on the shingle there utterly exhausted.

***Deduct 1 from your STRENGTH RATING. Go next to 166.***

### 336

A hideous piercing wail echoes round the swamp, causing even its mists to shudder, as the creature falls backwards into the slime. Its leathery fingers are still grasping the sword but you manage to prise it free. You then carry the cruel weapon back to the edge of the swamp so you can gouge out the massive diamond.

***Add 1 to the score on your TREASURE COUNTER. Now hurry well away from this region by going to 54.***

## 337

'Would you like another helping of meat?' the cook asks as you drop the book into your haversack. You wonder if you have selected the wrong one and this is his way of delaying you until Cragcliff's real bodyguards arrive. So you quickly take your leave of him, putting the cave a good distance behind you before examining the book. You quickly turn to the title page. There's a line of Latin across the top and underneath in much bigger lettering the three ornately-scribed words: *BOOK OF WISDOM*. You carefully put the volume into your haversack, knowing that its frail pages should greatly assist you on your quest.

*You may pick up the BOOK OF WISDOM CARD. Go next to 93.*

## 338

Keeping your writhing hostage in front of you, his neck in a python-like grip, you make your way to the goblet. But instead of drinking its contents, you contemptuously dash them to the floor. The prisoner watches in horror from his dangling chain. 'You fool,' he cries with as much force as his voice can muster. 'That potion could have greatly increased your strength. But I suppose you have done us prisoners a great favour in pouring it away. Now our torturers can't prolong our agony.' Before finally expiring for ever he feebly utters a few more words: 'Since you don't take my advice about the potion, at least take my advice now. Flee this dungeon immediately before any more torturers arrive.' *Go to 93.*

### 339

As you stride along this branch of the stepping-stones, you suddenly notice an inscription gouged into one of the stones. Some of the chiselled letters have been worn completely away and others are obliterated by crusts of rock-hard lichen, but those that are legible read: *O, Foolish one! It was one of the oth r branc es that you should have c osen. The mag c power of fores ght would have been g ven you there.* Realising how valuable this power would be on your quest, you decide to retrace your steps to the junction. But when you turn round you are startled to see that all the stepping-stones behind you have completely vanished. You have no choice but to continue forward. ***Go to 127.***

### 340

Giving a slight tug on the rudder, you steer your boat towards the middle arch. There's quite a strong current inside and you let this do the work for you, just occasionally steering the boat away from the tunnel's sides. You wonder when daylight is suddenly going to appear ahead, when these nightmare passages are finally going to end. You're sure that it can't be far now because you can begin to taste salt in the air. ***Go to 293.***

### 341

As you step on to the stone, you find that the glow is in fact caused by an ancient inscription gouged there; the fluorescent letters almost afire. It reads: *Darkness need be no more. Doubt need be no more. Whosoever stands on this stone shall have conferred on him the power of infra-red sight.* Realising what an asset such a power would be – enabling you to detect any dangers that lurk in patches of darkness – you praise the Fates for making you choose this particular route.

**You may pick up the INFRA-RED POWER card. Go next to 127.**

### 342

'Ah, you must be my new novice that the lord Cragcliff has sent me,' the old man assumes without turning round. 'You have come, am I right, to be taught some of my magic? Well, first, you must give me the password. My secrets are very special and I must be careful that they don't pass into the wrong hands. So tell me, youth, what is the correct password to receive my instruction.'

**If you have picked up the PASSWORD SCROLL in your adventure, use it here to find out the correct password. If you don't have the SCROLL, you'll have to guess the correct password.**

| If you think it's GARLON | **go to 47** |
| If you think it's TAGEL | **go to 168** |
| If you think it's RUTHLOR | **go to 301** |

*Other exciting titles in the Hodder and Stoughton Adventure Game Books series are:*

## FAMOUS FIVE ADVENTURE GAMES:

THE WRECKERS' TOWER GAME
THE HAUNTED RAILWAY GAME
THE WHISPERING ISLAND GAME
THE SINISTER LAKE GAME
THE WAILING LIGHTHOUSE GAME
THE SECRET AIRFIELD GAME
THE SHUDDERING MOUNTAIN GAME
THE MISSING SCIENTIST GAME

## ASTERIX ADVENTURE GAMES:

ASTERIX TO THE RESCUE
OPERATION BRITAIN

## THE PETER PAN ADVENTURE GAME:

PETER'S REVENGE

## BIGGLES ADVENTURE GAMES:

THE SECRET NIGHT FLYER GAME
THE HIDDEN BLUEPRINTS GAME

## THE FOOTBALL ADVENTURE GAME:

TACTICS!

## GHOST ADVENTURE GAMES:

GHOSTLY TOWERS
GHOST TRAIN

## WHO-DONE-IT ADVENTURE GAME:

SUSPECTS!